Free-Style CLASSICISM

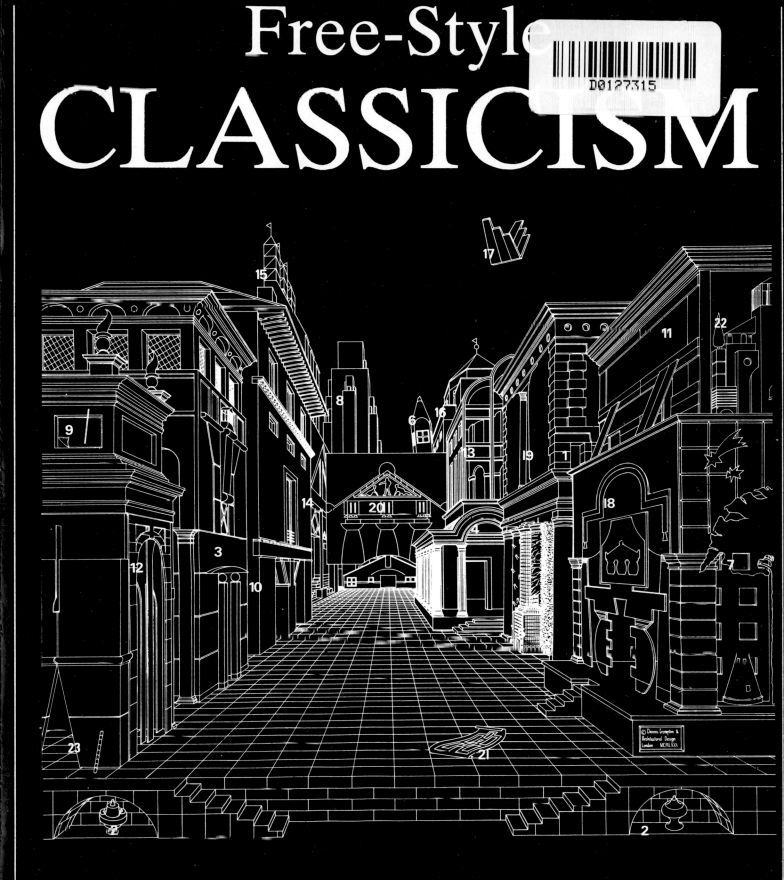

1 Ricardo Bofill/Taller de Arquitectura; 2 Studio GRAU; 3 Michael Graves; 4 Allan Greenberg; 5 Hans Hollein; 6 Charles Jencks; 7,8 Joseph Paul Kleihues; 9 Rem Koolhaas/OMA; 10 Leon Krier; 11 Arata Isozaki; 12 Charles Moore; 13 Paolo Portoghesi; 14 Franco Purini, Laura Thermes; 15 Aldo Rossi's Biennale gate; 16 Aldo Rossi's Teatro del Mondo; 17 Massimo Scolari; 18 Robert A M Stern; 19 Oswald Mathias Ungers; 20 Robert Venturi, John Rauch, Denise Scott Brown; 21 Georgio Benamo, Christian de Portzamparc; 22 Fernando Montes, Paris facade; 23 Christian de Portzamparc, Paris facade.

Michael Graves, Sunar Showroom ... ssicism (ph: Chas McGrath)

Free-Style
CLASSICISM

Guest-Edited by Charles Jencks

Free Style Classicism: The Wider Tradition Charles Jencks	**5**
Schinkel's Free-Style Pavilion Charles Moore	**22**
Five Lessons from Schinkel Oswald Mathias Ungers	**24**
The Ledoux Connection Arata Isozaki	**28**
Hans Hollein Haus Molag, Vienna	**30**
Chicago Post-Modern Classicism Charles Jencks	**32**
Aldo Rossi Modena Cemetery	**39**
Ricardo Bofill Palace of Abraxas	**42**
John Outram Terrace of Factories, London	**47**
Andrew Batey and Mark Mack Kirlin House and Holt House	**50**
Robert Mangurian and Craig Hodgetts South Side Settlement, Ohio	**54**
Takefumi Aida Toy Block House III, Tokyo	**58**
Robert Krier The White House, Berlin	**62**
Venturi, Rauch and Scott-Brown Brant House, Bermuda	**68**
Robert Stern Silvera Residence and Hitzig Apartment	**72**
Hanns Kainz and Associates Jessica McClintock Store, San Francisco	**76**
Moore, Grover, Harper Sammis Hall and Rudolph House	**80**
Charles Jencks Garagia Rotunda, Cape Cod	**84**
Jan Digerud and Jon Lundberg House Jessheim and Digerud Flat	**88**
Minoru Takeyama Nakamura Memorial Hospital, Sapporo	**92**
Kazuhiro Ishii Gable Building, Tokyo	**95**
Michael Graves San Juan Capistrano Library, and Sunar Showroom, LA	**98**
James Stirling, Michael Wilford and Associates The Clore Gallery, Tate Gallery, London	**102**
Free Style Orders Charles Jencks	**110**
A French Order: Ribart de Chamoust Charles Jencks	**113**
Representational Orders Charles Jencks	**117**

1   Christian de Portzamparc creates a hybrid of classicism and early modernism which many Europeans such as Rob Krier are attempting.
2   Hans Hollein, Museum of Glass and Ceramics, Teheran, 1977. Inside a restored Rococo room Hollein has collaged these display cases which are also giant light sources. Hollein shows respect for the classical tradition in extending it with modern materials and feelings.

3   S Urabe, Kurashiki City Hall, 1980, borrows quite literally from western civic symbolism, and then explodes it in size and graphic realism. The result is quite horrific to traditionalist eyes, a pastiche that would be rare even in Las Vegas. (ph: B Bognar)
4   Hiroshi Hara, in contrast, is all sobriety and sanctity, his houses always squeezed-together temples, where one finds absolute symmetry used in a hierarchic and mysterious way. (ph: B Bognar)

▲⊾ Architectural Design Profile

Acknowledgements

This *AD* Profile on Free Style Classicism — The Wider Tradition has been some time in preparation and is the result of many people's efforts if not continual collaboration. Arata Isozaki, Charles Moore and Oswald Mathias Ungers responded to my invitation to address the issues of Free Style and Pre-Modernists, while my students at UCLA and Pomona in Los Angeles and at the Architectural Association in London have designed Free Style orders. Other contributors, including the Japanese architects Ishii and Takeyama and the Norwegian architects Jan and Jon, have discussed the notion of Free Style; only Gerald Blomeyer takes exception to the label in his article on Rob Krier. In order to stitch together the texts and illustrations I have prefaced each project with a running commentary (in italics) and have written nearly all the captions (except where noted), but this should not imply that every one of the architects is in agreement with all the opinions expressed. I am grateful to all contributors for supplying material and finally wish to thank Ian Latham, Penelope Farrant and Richard Cheatle for constant editorial and design collaboration.

Charles Jencks

Editor and Publisher: Dr A C Papadakis

Published in Great Britain by Architectural Design, 7, Holland Street, London W8 as a part of AD 1-2/1982. Printed in Great Britain by Garden House Press.

Distributed in the USA by St Martin's Press, 175 Fifth Avenue, New York, NY 10010

Library of Congress Number 81-83704

ISBN (USA only) 0-312-30371-8

Charles Jencks
Free Style Classicism

The Wider Tradition

Many people are confused about the classical revival today, and this muddle is not confined to the general public or journalists. Architects are confused, experts are confused, classicists are confused and I hope to show there is good reason for this intellectual imbroglio. Today's classical revival is so unlike any other that it forces us to reassess the basic meaning of the term, to change the meaning of classicism, and it would be hard to find anything more disturbing than that for the meaning has been established for generations. In this essay classicism is defined broadly as a tradition more than a Greco-Roman style, a tradition which includes some periods, such as Gothic and Mannerist, which are often regarded as anti-classical. While some may consider this redefinition as too wide, it has the virtue of illuminating the ideas behind current Free Style Classicism, and the limits of classicism in general.

Old and New Definitions

John Summerson, in *The Classical Language of Architecture* (1963 re-edited 1980), sets out the conventional definitions which have held sway since the Renaissance. *'Classical architecture has its roots in antiquity, in the worlds of Greece and Rome ... the aim of classical architecture has always been to achieve a demonstrable harmony of parts ... And while we must incorporate these essentials (harmony and proportion) in our idea of what is classical we must also accept the fact that classical architecture is only recognisable as such when it contains some allusion, however slight, however vestigial, to the antique "orders".'*[1] This compound evocation (Summerson says: *'It is a mistake to try to define classicism'*) seems all right and it has been accepted by Helen Searing as the basis of her recent show on the kind of architecture we are also concerned with here. (**1, 2**) (The title of her exhibition is 'Speaking a New Classicism: American Architecture Now' and it is being held at Smith College and the Clark Art Institute in Massachusetts before travelling elsewhere.) Searing expands Summerson's potentially open 'definition' in the following way: *'Thus, by the "new classicism" we mean the presence in a given design of recognisably classical motifs (the orders, the aedicule), formats (the prostyle temple, the domed rotunda), and typologies (the Palladian villa, the Roman castra).'*[2] Again this seems a commonsense way of classifying recent developments as long as we don't enquire too deeply and ask more embarrassing questions: *'who* is recognising the motifs, *how many* formats or typologies must exist before we call a building classicist?'

By contrast, Helen Searing's co-author Henry Hope Read is much more strict in his definition confining it to straight revivalist buildings such as America's national Capitol. Reed is adamant that *'In architecture, the classical is identified not by proportions, nor by the plan, nor by materials, however important, but by ornament ... the human figure ... animal (lion mask and dolphin) and vegetable (acanthus and laurel) forms and ... this ornament is not Art Nouveau, nor Arabic, nor Egyptian, nor Gothic but Classical.'*[3] (**3**) However quaint this view of classicism seems, there are some architects willing to stand by it, and the implied 19th-century view is echoed by Summerson, who says: *'The porches of Chartres Cathedral are, in distribution and proportion, just about as classical as you can get, but nobody is ever going to call them anything but Gothic.'*[4] That may be quite true in a linguistic sense; we all follow conventions and the Gothic is not about to be overthrown. But, on a deeper level than social convention, don't the porches of Chartres accord with Summerson's own 'definition' – *'some allusion, however slight, however vestigial, to the antique "orders"*? They are certainly full of columns, 'harmony' and much of the animal,

1   Peter Hodgkinson and Taller Bofill, Church Sanctuary Meritxell, Andorra, 1974–80. Not 'Neo-Classicism' as commonly supposed but a Post-Modern classicism with hybrid references to many periods including the recent past. The black and white silhouette style owes as much to the 1920s as the Florentine Renaissance. Romanesque, Gothic and Modern constructional means are also mixed, but the resultant, sparse, flat image marks it of the present. (ph: Serena Vergano)

2   James Stirling, Portal, Staatsgalerie, Stuttgart, 1979 design, under construction. Simple demi-forms, the giant coved mouldings, intersect simplified classical signs; the squared pediment signifies a change from one exhibit to another. Note the way elements are collaged and eroded, the way the pediment slices the moulding; again these are recent Free Style devices not Neo-Classical ones. (ph: John Donat)

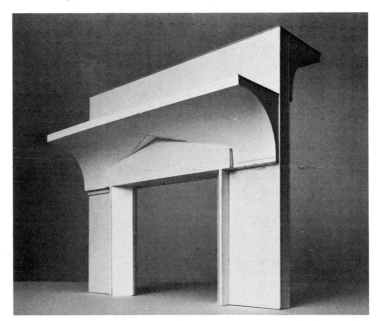

6 Karl Friedrich Schinkel, hallway, King Otto's palace project, Acropolis, Athens, 1834 (by kind permission of Colin St John Wilson)

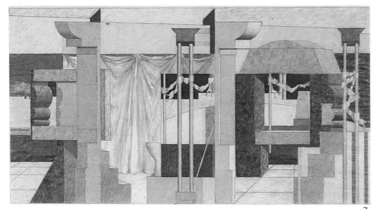

7   Michael Graves, *Alternative Landscape*, 1979. Graves' muted colours pull the eye past classical ribbons, drapery and travertine to a lonely landscape meant to provide respite for a claustrophobic room. Mediterranean pinks, blues and creams predominate.

8   Michael Graves, Portland Pavilion, USC Exhibition, Los Angeles, March 1981. Strong, flat polychromy accentuates the volumes while golds and blues accent the lighter members. The richer palette of Graves can be seen in the mural far right. This exhibition of paintings, drawings, models and designs showed the change from the dayglo colours of the Sixties, the tasteful pastels of the early seventies towards a more traditional opposition of saturated hues. (ph: C Jencks)

9   Thomas Gordon Smith, Tuscan and Laurentian Houses (left and right), Livermore, California, 1979–80. Picking up the polychromy of surrounding suburban buildings and a dark, Pompeian colouring Smith uses hues which have remained untouched by architects for a long time. Pastel tints of blue, rose, buff and yellow cover the walls while sculptural elements on the roof are picked out in darker green.

10   Edouart Loviot, Parthenon, Athens, restoration 1881, fourth Year envoi at the Ecole des Beaux Arts. Reds and blues almost vibrate, representational sculpture is also painted, the explicitness of imagery would be damned as kitsch were it done today. The Parthenon is not just the white architecture which Le Corbusier and the Neo-Classicists praised, but was a highly symbolic, polychromatic *mixed system* of languages. This mixture is the mark of a wider Free Style Classicism.

9

10

8

7

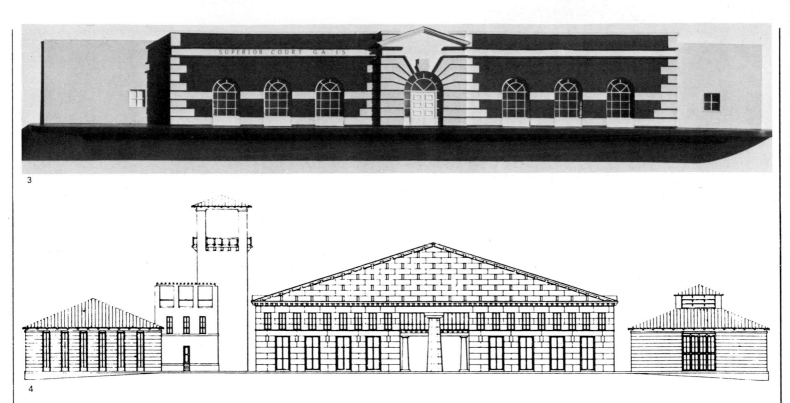

3

4

vegetable and human ornament which Henry Hope Reed finds necessary for the definition. If Summerson, later in his book, is going to allow Auguste Perret, Peter Behrens and Max Abramovitz into the back door of his classical pantheon, can he rightfully exclude a tradition which has so obviously evolved from the classical?[5] Indeed his own doubt is expressed in a double negative when he says of the classical and gothic: *'they are very different but they are not opposites and they are not wholly unrelated.'*[6] The further we push such questions the more we explore the contradictions in thought which have become conventionalised since the nineteenth century Battle of the Styles.

Other current theorists such as Demetri Porphyrios, who may be speaking for present classicists and some of the 'Rationalists', (**4**) defines the tradition as strictly as Reed but with, inevitably, another set of norms. He defined classicism in a symposium on the subject in December 1980 as *'the constructional logic of vernacular and its mimetic elaboration'*: for example, Doric elaborating some vernacular wooden details.[7] Again a set of 19th-century polarities – building versus architecture, necessity versus myth – are brought in to support a familiar argument. Porphyrios, like Reed, has the singular virtue in his canonic definition of excluding 95% of today's interesting classicism, a virtue pursued with some zest since he wants to keep his tradition pure and untainted by commerce, kitsch and, we might add, the reality principle. Indeed most classical revivals, including that of Vitruvius, have been movements of exclusion, and so it should be of no surprise that certain architects today wish to reassert some old taboos. They can find many precedents in the Renaissance, or with the Neo-Palladianism of Campbell or the Neo-Classicism of Laugier.

However helpful these purification rituals might be to the brotherhood of confirmed believers, they don't help us understand what classicism was in a wider sense, or what it is today. We have to look elsewhere for enlightenment. Helen Searing and Gavin Stamp have pointed out the current interest in looking at Romantic Classicists, a set of favoured architects from Ledoux to Schinkel, and they have put forward various theories to explain it: Modernism starts at this time, why not the new classicism? Stamp avers that this manner is the easiest style to copy and the least intellectually demanding.[8] But other periods and figures are in equal favour today: the Mannerists and Hawksmoor, the generation of 1900 and Lutyens, the Early Renaissance and Alberti – even, to introduce a doubt into this discussion, Egyptian, Romanesque, Baroque and Art Deco architects are studied with interest. No theorist or architect has yet been prepared to admit what may well be the truth: all periods of

architecture are being explored for their lessons and all of them have classicising elements.

Before the implications of this disarming pluralism are explored we might consider a few well-founded definitions of the subject outside architecture. The 11th edition of the Encyclopedia Britannica (1911) speaks for the informed opinion of that time when it focuses on the twin meanings of the classic as concerning 'authority' and 'Greece and Rome':

'The term "classic" is derived from the Latin epithet classicus, *found in a passage of Aulus Gellius (XIX.8.15) where a "*scriptor 'classicus'*" is contrasted with a "scriptor proletarius." The metaphor is taken from the division of the Roman people into* classes *by Servius Tullius, those in the first class being called* classici, *all the rest* infra classem, *and those in the last* proletarii. *The epithet "classic" is accordingly applied 1) generally to an author of the first rank, and 2) more particularly to a Greek or Roman author of that character.'*[9]

Hence in Western architecture the treatises which consider only the best of Greek and Roman architecture, or the canonic genealogies of design from Bramante to Palladio, or with Summerson's slightly expanded set, from Michelangelo to Borromini. These genealogies of design, reserved for the highest pedigree, make sense as far as they go.

But again a certain doubt may be introduced by pushing the analysis further. Suppose the tradition which starts with Greece, in the Doric, is continued to the recent past with, say, the 'Doric' of 'the first rank' Mies van der Rohe and his allusions 'however slight, however vestigial', to the antique 'orders' (**5**). No one will deny that Mies produced a kind of Schinkelesque classicism when young and then transformed it into a kind of modern Doric I-beam order when older, but some will dispute bitterly that this has anything of

3   Allan Greenberg, Court House, Manchester, Conn, 1978–80. A near straight revival of classicism although innovations can be noted: the flat facade is accentuated by two 'string courses' that pull away from the corner quoins. The centre arched doorway also introduces minor surprises into a generalised language. Lutyens, whom Greenberg admires, also developed such a second glance architecture.

4   Leon Krier, School for 500 Children, St Quentin-en-Yvelines, France, 1977–9. Vernacular and classical styles are mixed in a way which recalls what Porphyrios has termed 'Doricism' – that is a mixture of archetype, constructional image, minimum shelter and monument. Although at first the buildings may appear normalised there are certain features, such as the heavy Doric column in the centre or the absent base, which break the normal canons of classicism. The emphasis on stereometry as an expression of construction is typical of the Fundamentalist Free Style. The result is noble if a bit severe for children.

5

6

importance to do with Greek architecture or the deeper classical tradition; Norris Kelly Smith is one:

'I do not mean to suggest that the measured and impersonal style of Mies and his imitators can be regarded as a modern equivalent of the traditional classicism that descends from the Greek temple. While it possesses something of the formal purity and objectivity of that style, it quite lacks the relationship to the word which is essential to the humanising significance of the ordered architecture of the past. Whereas every part of the Greek temple, . . . has its own distinctive form, belongs to a class of similar and interchangeable parts, and can be identified by name, the Miesian building consists only of rectangles – shapes that have little relation to the human body and which do not come together, in a work such as the Seagram Building, to constitute a society of members, as do the parts of the Parthenon.'[10]

Here we again have the characteristic problem of definition. Certain things are taken to be essential to classicism which are not discovered in the building at hand and so it is excluded from the canon. That the 'canon' or 'classic' is variably defined across time tends to be overlooked by the definers of each generation. In reviewing my *Post-Modern Classicism* (AD 5/6 1980), Nicholas Penny, a classical scholar and co-author of *Taste and the Antique*, adopts the typical essentialist position:

'From a new Classicism one has the right to expect a system of ideal proportions, certainly lucidity and harmony of plan and elevation, but there is less evidence of this in the buildings that are the book's subject than there was when the Modern Movement was in full swing. As for monumentality, which one would also expect, it is certainly attempted at Les Arcades du Lac, the glum pre-cast concrete new town by Ricardo Bofill which includes some painfully ungainly cylinders and triangles ... There is no evidence here of any serious desire to revive the solemnity or the grandeur of the ancient stone architecture...'[11] [my emphasis]

The essentials Penny expects to find thus differ from those of Summerson, Searing, Porphyrios and Reed, some of the other authorities we have looked at. There may be overlap in their judgement – Greece and Rome remain as a common definer – and perhaps they might agree on some mutual view of classical and non-classical buildings, but when they come to define it they look for different essentials, and with considerably different taste and assumptions. The straight revivalism of Reed has little to do with the 'slight allusions' of Summerson and Searing which has little in common with the severe Doric of Porphyrios, and so on. We might conclude in exasperation that the word 'classical' is even more

hopeless than 'romantic', a concept which has already been subjected to historical dismemberment into its variable meanings.[12] Should we give it up because of its permissive vagueness; or keep it for its evocative power since it can mean something to everyone? Clearly there are choices other than these.

Before we look at them we might focus on Nicholas Penny's distaste for Post-Modern Classicism and Bofill's work in particular, because this uneasiness is shared by some other critics who have a taste for 18th-century classicism. Basically the work of Bofill is being excluded from their canon not because it lacks their essentials (ideal proportion, harmony, monumentality and grandeur it does have), but because it is crudely done in comparison with the pre-existing canon (**6**). It is done in concrete not stone, with heavy pre-cast walls and not delicate, sculpted pilasters. In a word it is *proletarii* not *classici*, or for the 'masses not the classes' – a phrase that apparently perturbed Penny.

Here we touch upon another shift in the concept of classicism which is starting to get underway. A few architects are using new materials, outside the canonic stone, wood and stucco, like neon and stainless steel which are associated with mass culture, and they are also designing buildings for the *proletarii*. This, in a style previously used mostly by the upper class for banks, clubs, country houses and places of civic grandeur violates a still powerful taboo. But even if we probe this we can see its arbitrary nature; after all the style was also used in that most canonic building of all, where Christians were slaughtered for amusement, the colosseum. If one looks more closely at Greek and Roman architecture than in their idealism, the classical revivalists have done, a richer picture

5   Mies van der Rohe, Crown Hall, IIT, Chicago 1962. Describable in classical terms as a temple carried by four large trusses and seventeen I-beams, a major and minor order of construction, with a 'base', *'piano nobile'* and architrave (no cornice). The building also lacks several classical features: polychromy, ornament, conventional symbolism, statuary and a 'named' set of parts. If we add up the classical features then we might conclude that the building is Free Style classical; but if we look at Mies' intention then we would judge it otherwise. (ph: C Jencks)

6   Ricardo Bofill, Les Arcades du Lac, St Quentin-en-Yvelines, France, 1976–80. Precast arcades, pediments and 'pilasters' brought in by travelling crane, columns of earth colour tiles, a heavy and basic classicism meant for mass housing. The results are superior to most low cost estates, the image and space are exhilarating if somewhat rigid and grandiose. For such creations Bofill has aroused more than the usual condescension due to the grand scheme and perhaps this is caused by a certain guilty conscience over mass-housing. In spite of such contempt I believe in several years Bofill will be welcomed for having brought together such seemingly incompatible traditions: classicism, mass production and mass-housing.

emerges than the expurgated one. Ancient classicism was always a mixed symbolic system, partly high-minded and abstract, partly vulgar and representational, partly applied to the temples on high, and partly used in the market-place and brothel.

Classicism, as a living language of architecture today, is just as involved with the new technologies, the vulgate and *prolatarii* as the Greeks and Romans were: that is somewhat involved. When Charles Moore uses steel volutes on his capitals, his 'imitations' are no less nor more vulgar than those of Callimachus who copied acanthus leaves in bronze. The vibrating reds and blues, the strong almost day-glo colours which some attribute to the Parthenon are mirrored by the violent colours of Thomas Gordon Smith or the rich colours of Michael Graves, colours unpalatable to many tastes developed by white Modernism and white classicism. (**7, 8, 9, 10**)

So we have a slight shift in meaning today as classicism becomes more democratic and involved with the social reality of building for different tastes and cultural levels. We find an aspect which has always been inherent in its claims for universality: it can modify archetypal patterns to suit local conditions, building materials and meaning. The wider tradition of classicism, in spite of the authorities, includes Gothic.

Classicism as Tradition and Essence
Once we admit Gothic as a sub-class of this genre then along come a host of other styles for inclusion: Roman*esque*[13] is clearly part of the main family as are Mannerism, Baroque and Rococo because of their elaboration of some classical tropes. After this the more unpedigreed styles can be related to the main bloodline: Art Nouveau Classicism (eg, Otto Wagner), Art Deco Classicism (eg, Raymond Hood) and the current Post-Modern Classicism. Other styles may be contrasted with it: Expressionism and Constructivism. Finally it can be seen in a new historical context as a continuously changing language which has evolved from the Egyptians and Assyrians.

Here is another fundamental shift in our definition and one obviously related to the egalitarian and pluralist shifts we have just noted. Instead of Greece and Rome being the sole originators of the style we can now see that most of the salient features have evolved from Egyptian architecture: a monumental building of continuous, smooth stone having several ornamented orders based on different vegetable and animal metaphors, with much of the articulations of subsequent classicism. Stylobate, abacus, echinus, fluting, architrave, frieze, cornice, and on a suprasegmental level – anthropomorphic proportion, grid planning, simple harmonies, axes and cross axes, elementary addition of functional units are the main classical features which the Greeks learned from the Egyptians (**11**). A future definition of classical architecture, as opposed to classical music and literature, may have to recognise this fundamental historical evolution and relatively diminish the role of Greece and Rome. At least this would be true if counting stylistic motifs and architectural ideas were all that is involved in classification. It is nevertheless more complex than this: the relative importance of ideas is basic to our definitions of classicism and these include several notions which may act like the essence of the style.

Before we try to adjudicate between motif counting and essentialism, or take up the old philosophical argument of realists versus nominalists, the current implications of the debate should be noted for it is these which have sparked off the need for a reassessment. Architects, as pointed out, have started to look at all classical periods of architecture, not just Mannerism and Neo-Classicism, and thus the stylistic references may be placed in different epochs. For instance Michael Graves' Portland Building (**12**) has a black podium and arcade which tends to be seen in America as Art Deco and Egyptian (deriving its heavy blocks from the solid square piers of the river temples); in Europe, because of other associations, it is seen as related to Neo-Classicism, the Fascist architecture of the Thirties or the work of Aldo Rossi and Leon Krier. With Graves we know that all of these references are possible for he looks to many periods for inspiration. With Japanese designers, and even those I have characterised as Fundamentalist, the heterogeneity of reference is wide, if not equally so. Takefumi Aida (**13**) uses classical fragments in his Building Block Building – square attic window,

triangular pediment and central column – which might be derived equally from Eastern and Western sources (he is acquainted with both), but he recombines these elements in a fundamentalist and childlike way that is distinctly his own. Thus the precise source is lost or generalised to the classical tradition as a whole. Likewise Andrew Batey and Mark Mack summarise an heterogeneous set of classical (and other) sources which are universalised through reduction to an archetype (**14**). Their Stewart Houses derive, as other work, from Roman courtyard houses, Egyptian wall architecture, Lluis Baragon and here, specifically, the Los Angeles courtyard houses of Irving Gill. The strong symmetry and central axis, as in Aida's work, is combined with very simple Renaissance harmonies and rhythms to produce an image that is, in the classical phrase, 'timeless' (although we know only certain times prefer this ascetic aesthetic).

We could multiply this heterogeneity of sources indefinitely, but the point is probably accepted that Post-Modern Classicisms may revive, or learn from, any period which has developed the classicist archetypes (arch, dome, order etc). This eclecticism of sources is a counterpart to the egalitarianism of the movement as well as a result of present day travel and scholarship which have, in a sense, equalised different periods. Perhaps the influence of current media should not be overemphasised, but architectural magazines, excellent and inexpensive histories of architecture, and the architects' extensive and growing slide collections have, in one way, collapsed time and space so that we may feel very familiar with Ancient Greece while not being able to speak its language. The fashionable way to dismiss this as 'consumption of the image' misses the important point that the image is, in the best case, absorbed and transformed by the architect into one of his linguistic means – as we have just seen with Graves, Aida, Batey and Mack.[14]

Central to the argument for a *tradition* of Free Style Classicism (rather than just a Greco-Roman style) is one idea of a form-model or theme. We classify, at the crudest level, by counting the number of themes which can be statistically correlated with other members of a class. Thus if a Romanesque building has ten of fifteen major classical themes we might place it in the corpus. To a degree this is what biologists do with their method of 'numerical taxonomy': compute the taxons, identifiable characterisics, to see how related one species is to another.[15] On a more traditional level of building it is simply noting the concurrent transformations of several architectural themes across time. The idea of the engaged column and its relation to the wall, floor and entablature may be traced from Egypt to the present day. If this theme persists, and if enough of them persist, we may speak of a continuous architectural tradition – Free Style Classicism. Furthermore, as a consequence, we may also speak of a cluster of such ideas which are greatly important and which constitute several models of the Western facade. These may be treated as *essential types*, the major themes of the tradition: the arch/dome; the street/doorway/facade; the Orders; the colosseum/palazzo; the temple/gable/aedicule. (**15, 16**)

---

11 J B Fischer von Erlach, *Entwurf einer historischen Architektur*, 1721. A Theban pyramid of Fischer combines, as much of his own work does, themes taken from the wider history of classicism starting with the Egyptian and Babylonians. The hybrid classicism reminds one of the later mixtures of Ledoux and Lequeu equally striking for their monumentality, symbolism and juxtaposition. Fischer, above all, could see the classical tradition whole, as a large family, and he was one of the last to attempt a synthesis of disparate cultures united by common archetypes.

12 Michael Graves, Portland Public Services Building, Portland, 1980–82. Black 'Egyptian' base rather like Hatshepsut's Mortuary Temple. The pyramidal massing and volumetric heaviness also recall this era, although others have seen Art Deco, Neo-Classical and Fascist overtones. The building is intended to be multivalent.

13 Takefumi Aida, Building Block Building II, Yokohama, 1979. Classical symmetries, square attic windows, pitched roof and implied palazzo order are offset by Japanese references such as the central ridge pole support. Shintoism and Classicism are often combined by this supreme metaphysician. (ph: Botond Bognar)

14 Andrew Batey and Mark Mack, Stewart House, Pasadena, 1978–80. Aside from relating to the local work of Gill and Schindler this courtyard house has the absolute symmetry, axiality and frontality of an Egyptian mortuary temple. The architects have developed their primitivist 'wall' architecture from Roman houses and the work of Barragon, a typical Post-Modern hybridisation that parallels OMA'a combination 'Suprematist Pompei'.

11

12

13

14

15

16

Perhaps one reason for the present classical revival is explained simply by architects rediscovering these archetypes after they had been censored for so long. The themes amount to a type of architectural 'truth' rather like the mathematical kind, midway between invention and discovery. This is a classical notion itself and one which has led to the ideal of universality, an ideal which may have been overdone in the past as certain 'universal' forms were applied indiscriminately, but, as engineers will admit, there are only a few intelligent ways of designing the wheel. The essential types of architecture are also limited and classicism has taken out its patent on a number of them. Furthermore we might add that the essence of classicism, historically speaking, consists in achieving a balance between several such archetypes and the contradictory codes of architecture so that the balance represents, if not the harmonious integration always claimed, the idea of including opposite elements: ornament and representation, sculptural plasticity and architectonic order, urban propriety and appropriate functional expression. The list of antitheses could go on until it reached one of the final classical polarities – truth versus beauty – the argument between the naturalism of Michelangelo and the aesthetic order of Raphael which E H Gombrich has found to characterise so much classical art.[16] Or it could be seen as a natural working out of the contradictory demands which Vitruvius and the classical tradition put on the art; that is mediating between 'firmness, commodity and delight' or in modern terms 'technic, function and form'. On the most general level we could hazard our definition: the essence of classicism is to include opposite codes of architecture in such a way that none of its contradictory demands are altogether sacrificed. The wider tradition of classicism *conventionally* included opposite codes: not only the Vitruvian triad but painting, sculpture, ornament, polychromy and on other levels political ideology, social aspirations, and urban ordering principles. In this sense much Neo-Classicism was anti-classical.

If one accepts the redefinition of a wider classicism being proposed, which is egalitarian as well as upper class, Egyptian as well as Greco-Roman and inclusivist at its heart, then the next pressing question concerns the limitations to this expanded category. How do we distinguish buildings which have just one or two classical motifs from the Free-Style tradition? It is partly a question of statistical balance and partly of intention. Toyo Ito's house in Chuo-Rinkan uses thin modern material such as aluminium and steel which are not classical in feeling but he then puts them together according to classical compositional principles in plan and elevation, and he uses identifiable motifs such as the pediment, truss, barrel vault, lattice cross and symmetrically placed window

shutters (**17, 18**). The free style intention is clear because so many classical ideas are accentuated. By contrast Seiichi Shirai, in his Shinwa Bank, may use classical elements such as the post and lintel and round *oeil de boeuf*, but he does so in a context which is mainly intended to disarm the viewer through Surrealist juxtaposition and violent scale distortion (**19**). Classical fragments are used for non-classical ends: disharmony, inappropriate juxtaposition, cultural dislocation (ends which are not necessarily negative as they sound). In order to make such distinctions between classical and non-classical one has to impute different intentions to the architecture and one cannot rely on formal analysis alone.[17] It thus becomes a matter of weighing the evidence, of balancing one idea and form against another.

To sum up the implications of Free Style Classicism we may say it is a wide tradition not confined to the Greco-Roman alone (although that may be the heart of the tradition). It is a changing body of theory and practice which keep a set of themes developing, not as in the case of the Straight Revivalists, an application of static formulae. It is a tradition which acknowledges the authority of precedent and the discovery of architectural truths, but it hardly regards those discovered as the final ones and it seeks the extension of these by engaging the emergent social reality, using new materials, and developing new rhetorical tropes. In a word it is a living tradition full of faults and promise.

15 The Hephaisteion, Athens, 449–444 BC. The classic Doric temple rendered in its typicality and idealism. The pedimental end is a logical expression of the interior truss and, as a design idea, signifies the cross section of the temple, the frontality of entrance and repetition of trabeation. The pediment thus becomes the conventional sign of this type and remains the signifier of temple and Greek architecture long after it is transformed into other types (below). (ph: C Jencks)

16 Joseph Cather Newsom, 1425 Miramar Street, Los Angeles, 1890. Transformation of the the temple pediment in a local language. Here Newsom wanted to design the typical 'Californian' mansion and he uses the pediment idea at several scales – as aedicular entrance, balcony and gable – in a way which has nothing to do with the trabeated temple. Free Style Classicism is based on the transformation of ideas across cultures and building types. (ph: C Jencks)

17, 18 Toyo Ito, House in Chuo-Rinkan, Japan, 1980. Greek pediment, Roman barrel vault and cross-bracing, symmetrical plan on second floor – these classical elements are realised with a thin modern technology and small scale delicacy one associates particularly with Japanese houses. As in much of Ito's work there is a very cool treatment of the surface, almost a cold intellectual quality that recalls the Mannerism of Michelangelo. (ph: Tomio Ohashi)

19 Seiichi Shirai, Shinwa Bank, Sasebo, 1976. Heavy columnar walls, steel post, lintel and *oeil de boeuf* – classical allusions but Surrealist intentions. Shirai often reduces Western motifs to a simple formula and then explodes the scale to bring out their incongruity. Thus classical motifs are used for non-classical ends. (ph: Botond Bognar)

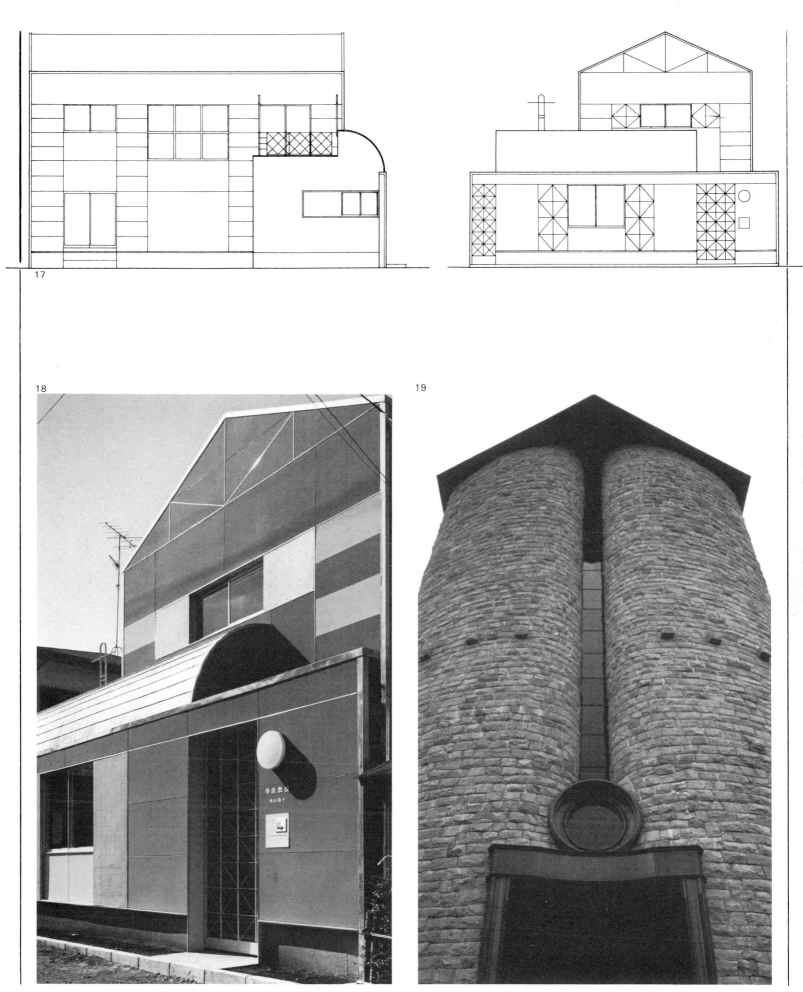

17

18

19

Canonic versus Free Style

Inherent in Post-Modern Classicism is a basic division which gives a certain life to the movement: that is the dialectic between canonic and rule-breaking classicism. In the past such divisions amounted to an argument over Vitruvius and later Palladio. The Ancients versus the Moderns, the code-enforcing perfectionists versus the code-extending innovators, was the most obvious dichotomy. Perhaps one should be wary of such binary oppositions when architectural reality is a continuous scale of differences, but still there is something to be learned by a simple antithesis. Thus we might divide up the classical architectural world between canonic and Free Style designers. The former emphasise the setting up and enforcement of canons, or rules, in order to ensure a successful building and to refine details towards greater beauty and suitability (**20**). They obviously include such figures as Vitruvius, St Bernard (in so far as he influenced building), Brunelleschi, Alberti, Palladio, Scamozzi, Bellori, F Mansart, Lord Burlington, Campbell, Gibbs, Laugier, Jacques-Francois Blondel, Winckelmann, Cordemoy, Durand and many 18th- and 19th-century French teachers. Perhaps many on this short list would disagree with each other, but they would take even greater exception to the licenses of the following: Imhotep (very free style), Hadrian (criticised for designing 'pumpkin domes'), Charlemagne (producer of Free Style versions of Ravenna architecture), Abbot Suger (who introduced gaudy stained glass) and then the more usual characters Serlio, Michelangelo, Borromini, De Vries, Dietterlin, Ledoux, Le Queu, Labrouste, Schinkel and Latrobe.

This basic opposition could be continued to the present and we would find a similar distinction between the Fundamentalists – Aldo Rossi, Leon Krier, Mark Mack, Reinhardt and Reichlin, Hodgetts and Mangurian, and Thomas Beeby (**21**) – and the Historicists – Michael Graves, Robert Venturi, Jeremy Dixon, Robert Stern, Paolo Portoghesi, and Charles Moore (**22**). The former, again, seem to regard the setting up and observance of canons to be the most important while the latter regard the extension, inversion and re-use of fixed conventions as significant. Given the natural tensions between these two approaches it is quite usual for an architect to opt for one or the other; but with historical hindsight and the present pluralism in mind we can have the luxury of accepting both as positive. Indeed on further investigation of the links between them it would appear that in order to understand one side the other must be perceived. To appreciate rule-breaking innovations one has to have a deep respect for the rules, and to see that the new rules are set up on the reformulation of the old ones also entails this double view.

The Fundamentalists who stick very closely to materials, construction, city rules, archetypes and functions as they narrowly define them create conventions which the Historicists often assume as they extend them. Why there should be such basic divides in the history of architecture may not be a question we have to ask since we set up the polarity in the first place and mentioned that there were many intermediary figures (de L'Orme, Vasari, Bernini, Chambers, Soane, or today Hollein, Stirling and Isozaki (**23**)). Nevertheless we can point to certain psychological traits which make these groups distinct, and trace historical strands which bind them together. Indeed E H Gombrich has shown in his essay 'Norm and Form' that many of those architects or theorists cited here in the canonic tradition simply transformed Vitruvius' censure of his 'irrationalists' into their censure of the 'free stylists'.[18] Vasari against Gothic, Bellori against Borromini, Winckelmann against the Rococo and, we might add, Campbell against the Baroque, or today Porphyrios and Krier against Moore and Venturi – they wheel out the classical gun of constructional realism and let fly, as Vitruvius did, against anything which does not fit their narrow canons. We may smile when such old battles recur again today, but what is more cause for ironic surprise is the strange case of the free stylist who espouses absolute canons. We will look at such a case, John Soane, in the later discussion of Free Style orders, and only remark here that such a contradiction is a natural consequence of the duality we have mentioned that constitutes a dual unity. Canonic versus Free Style? They're really only opposed polemically.

20 Christian Heinrich Grosch, The University, Oslo, 1841–52. A Greek Ionic portico leads to a Doric hall. The scheme, striving for a normalised or classic solution which nevertheless combines different functional and symbolic elements, was sent to K F Schinkel for his comments, and thus several motifs were perfected: the Ionic capital, the grand portico with its triple height space and sculptural stairway dividing it up. (ph: C Jencks)

21 Bruno Reichlin and Fabio Reinhardt, Casa Sartori, Ticino, Switzerland, 1975–77. The vernacular 'wall' architecture of the area punctured by an axial fan light which accents the front door and its asymmetrical placement. The implied pediment relates to other modern villas in the vicinity. Like Aldo Rossi, who has influenced these architects, very simple forms are set in a slightly new and disquieting relationship. Thus wall, 'pediment' and fan light are elided together to produce an 'unfinished' whole. Although the forms are used in their archetypal generality, the canonic semi-circle, etc, their combination is Free Style. (ph: B Reichlin)

22 Charles Moore and Richard Chylinski, *Moore, Rogger, Hofflander Condominium*, Los Angeles, 1978. Extreme distortion of classical and vernacular themes. The exaggerated monopitch roof indicates the diagonal stair apartment; chimney elements are reminiscent of Moore's favourite American classic – Stratford Hall, 1725. The fanlight theme is broken apart twice and used as a fragment. To appreciate these distortions fully one must know the canonic forms to which they refer. (ph: C Jencks)

23 Arata Isozaki, Fukuoka-Sogo Bank, Home Offices, Fukuoka, 1972. A Modernist slab and Renaissance palazzo are mixed in this apparently straightforward building. The giant four columns and beam set up a Mannerist relationship as the 'absent' capital is indicated by the gap between shaft and architrave. Isozaki manages to combine the canonic and Free Style, straight and crooked elements of classicism. (ph: Masao Arai)

24   25   26

Some New Rhetorical Figures

If Free Style Classicism plays with canonic conventions, it does so with the idea that a living language has to operate somewhere between the Scylla of predictability and the Charybdis of the totally new. Between the cliché of Straight Revivalism and the neologism of the avant-garde is an expanding area, a new Post-Modern Classical style which architects such as Michael Graves are in the process of creating. We explored, in the previous *AD Profile* on the subject, a few of the rhetorical figures that are emerging – *personification, paradox, elision* and *archetype* – and to these must be added many more. In the confines of this issue, however, we will examine only four.

A recurring figure which many Post-Modernists use is *erosion*. The sudden cutting away of a wall area to reveal another wall behind, which in turn may be cut away (or transparent), is characterisic of so much recent work that in truth we have to see it as a general idea of our time made possible by recent technologies. Thus Late-Modernists such as Richard Meier will erode the corners and floors of his buildings just as will Robert Venturi. Nonetheless erosion as a conscious rhetorical figure, exaggerated as such, is more typical of Post-Modernists.

Hanns Kainz uses eroded rustication in a way which is traditional, alternating voussoirs as quoins used to alternate, but also original: now the smaller quoins are made into thin voids (**24**). The overall eroded figure here is that of a triumphal arch, or Serliana (ABA), again a conventional figure for entryway, but one which has been given a startling new twist. Kainz is thus playing here on the fact that a conventional masonry sign of door can be signified by its absence (the ghost image) and the absence behind it (the plane of glass held by metal clips, which in our culture has come to be recognised as a door). This play of appearance versus reality is taken up in the realistic mannikins to either side, and indeed the whole boutique on the inside where further aspects of *trompe l'oeil* are exploited. By sectioning the cantilevered concrete voussoirs and showing us the literal constructional reality Kainz further exaggerates the difference between representation and fact. It is rather as if a Neo-Classicist were to pull back the curtain of his marble veneer to reveal the vernacular concrete or wood.

Jan Digerud and Jon Lunberg, two Norwegian architects, have designed several floors of offices using many classical figures which are eroded (**25**). Here again the ghosts of forms we know well are left by solid planes; particularly the triangular and segmental pediment. The functional idea behind this was quite explicit: to create many individual subdivided places out of similar office floors which would allow defined centres as well as an ease of communication between them. Each floor is thus divided into what they conceive as a *cardo* and *decumanus*, main Roman cross streets; then on further minor streets classical aedicules are placed. Here we find the common 'door' to three offices pivoting as an erosion around a central pier. The silhouette 'pediments' are broken – an Art Deco stagger in one case and Baroque fracture in the other two. Since the ghost figure is rather complex the white material is kept simple and the reference planes are continued in plan. The resultant space is the conventionalised one of Post-Modernism: layered, complex, full of demi-forms, ambiguity and surprise. It is interesting that such space is now being used in a building task where the isotropic space of Late-Modernism, that open office planning, had a great success. Digerud and Lundberg as well as the client, a university publishing house, don't hide the fact that the employees prefer it to *Bürolandschaft*.

Erosion is combined, literally, with the demi-form in Robert Stern's Hitzig apartment to create one half the silhouette of a squat Doric column with a double abacus (**26, 27**). The obvious reference is to Labrouste's drawings of sectioned columns at Paestum, an image that is here used to increase the sense of space, and amusement, in a claustrophobic New York corridor which has no exterior window. The way the 'absent' column turns into a thin line at the base distinguishes the curved partition from the pre-existing wall. A further series of figures unites while dividing the two halves: curved moulding versus flat one, discontinued 'frieze' moulding versus 'cornice'. Back lighting above the eroded 'frieze' gives a feeling of extended space as it does many times in the Norwegian offices. Clearly the use of erosion and the silhouette figure has an economic rationale in an age which doesn't want to spend money on real columns and Serliana, and some people may want to read these figures for their psychological attributes: they express our anxieties about the past and our fear of the present when the only thing left to us is an 'absence', a hole. Such deeper meanings do however conflict with the superficial ones which are intended, so obviously, to amuse. The conflict, if it exists, has also been read into Mannerist buildings.

24   Hanns Kainz, Jessica McClintock Store, San Francisco, 1981. Two figures are eroded from the front – the Serliana and rusticated quoins. Then the glass wall, indicated by clips and reflective surface, provides a further layering. Note the way the keystone turns into an Art Deco Z-shape and quoins become voussoirs. (ph: C Jencks)

25   Jan Digerud and Jon Lundberg, University Publishers, Oslo, 1980. Four doors are eroded from these offices to leave a central pier and silhouette of broken pediments. Functionally the erosion works to unify the divided offices and provide for surprising, oblique views. (ph: C Jencks)

26, 27   Robert Stern, Hitzig Apartment, New York, 1979–80. A 'Doric' column is eroded from half of the partition and existing wall to allow light and space to flow through these tight, claustrophobic areas. Another paradoxical figure is set up by repeating the white mouldings at different scale and then running them across divided areas. The idea of the aedicule, or little house within the house, is reinforced by the small table. (ph: Stoecklin)

28, 29   Robert Venturi and John Rauch, Faculty Club, Penn State University, Philadelphia, 1974–76. Many familiar elements are used here in a slightly unfamiliar way: the house image is amplified, the hunting lodge is miniaturised, the windows have their domestic scale increased, trellis is used with smaller than usual openings (and hangs). The chairs, light bulbs and shingle remain a normal size to accentuate distortions.

27
28
29

30

There is more obvious motivation in our next two categories – *amplification* and *miniaturisation* – which are complementary rhetorical devices which allow a double reading. In the Pennsylvania Faculty Club Venturi and Rauch have amplified a domestic form, the pitched roof house, so that the faculty can eat, as it were, under one domestic roof. Window openings and mullion dimensions are increased, details are simplified, a light green trellis screen hangs above the head indoors, out of context (**28, 29**). These odd distortions of convention (even the 'institutional green' is 'off') are not meant to annoy or shock so much as to gently nudge one into looking again at the familiar. In this case several familiar images are partly combined: nave and aisle organisation, garden room and, on the outside, large country house or hunting lodge. Thus amplification is tied to a calculated ambiguity to produce an ambivalent image that almost fits into many categories. Presumably this follows the ethic of the architects that things, like Main Street, 'are almost all right' (or always a little wrong, to put the same thing differently).

It's probably obvious from the foregoing that one man's ampli-fication is another man's miniaturisation; it depends partly on the visual codes of the viewer which of these two possibilities is perceived. Does increasing the scale of the window mullions and panes make the windows look bigger than normal, and the Faculty Club smaller, as I would expect; or is the building seen as a large hunting lodge shrunken down. Such issues are particularly important to mass housing that is really massive – the 19-storey 'palaces' of Ricardo Bofill – which are made to look like three-storey 'houses' (see his project in Marne below). Negatively such scale dislocations may heighten the sense of density and overcrowding – if they are perceived as increasing the size.

For a Zen Temple in Japan, Monta Mozuna has amplified an aedicule to become a kind of baldachino (an old idea) or, according to another reading, he has shrunk a temple to 'house' the statues (**30**). The actual structure has the further uncanny quality of looking like a model or doll's house. Thus dislocations in scale are being combined with changes in texture to heighten the sacred realm. The fact that Western classical forms appear to be used – Laugier's primitive hut of four columns on a square – may be again only partly intended as in other Japanese work. Zen, as a philosophy, plays on the rhetorical figure of paradox both for its heuristic potential and metaphysical meaning. Knowing that Mozuna likes to mix incompatible metaphysical systems to show their hidden compatibility leads one to suppose that both he and Zen priests have intended the set of visual paradoxes.

A quick paradox, *oxymoron*, is another key rhetorical tool for intensifying the experience of a building. By including opposites, in close proximity, a feeling of uneasiness or tension is created which leads the eye and mind to search elsewhere for release or understanding. Mangurian and Hodgetts have combined several near opposites in the 'false front' entrance to a theatre or meeting room (**31**). Here the contradictions 'wall/niche', 'flat/curved', 'impenetrable/punctured' are set up by concrete block that is itself used like paper (in tension across the top). The idea of an exedra framed by paired columns is faintly recalled here, as is the traditional Christian apse and triumphal arch. As with Venturi's ambiguous allusions one is not quite sure of the building type being evoked here, or even the period of architecture (is it Early Roman or Late Kahn?). In any case the use of oxymoronic signs is probably appropriate for a ceremonial entrance to a theatre (which is now only lacking its stairway leading to the balcony). If and when the artist Alice Aycock builds this grand *escalier* in wood the false front will serve its symbolic purpose, the route will have its frame.

31

The Taller de Arquitectura and Ricardo Bofill have designed a 'roofless roof' for the transformation of a Romanesque sanctuary (**32**). This paradox is created by extending the arches from the building into the outdoor cloister – a repetition which can be clearly perceived to underline the inherent distinction 'roofed/unroofed'. Parabolic arches, also white on black, make the sign even more obvious. And what does this paradoxical 'arch which doesn't carry' do? It obviously frames a view of the Andorra mountains, or the sky, and therefore defines the sacred realm both inside the sanctuary *and* nature beyond.

For a studio in Cape Cod I have designed the 'domeless dome' which acts as the Meritxell arches do to frame the sky (**33**). This figure may be related to the oculus, the 'eye' of the Pantheon, and it certainly acts in a similar way to send a circular light spot around the building during the day. But the specific idea was to create a reference to the four horizons and the significant natural features (ocean, pond, hill, slope) and mark them with four axial features. Thus the steps of the trellis act, as they do in Palladio's Villa Rotonda, to point from the centre to landscape; but here the curved dome, only one-inch thick, combined with the thin trellis members, mocks the usage of this sacred form in private villas. The Pantheon dome had a sacred significance until Palladio brought it into the private realm. Thus the 'domeless dome' and 'stepless steps' try to have it both ways – as cosmic symbols and cheap sunshades.

32
33

In all these rhetorical figures we may discern a double intention that verges on irony. The idea of using a classical language for its beauty and commonality is combined with the idea of sending quite new messages. An harmonious aesthetic is included here, but it is combined with things which may be experienced as 'ugly'. Post-Modernists appeal to society at large with its expectancies, and to an elite group which includes themselves. The compound classicism which is the result of this double-coding exists in other periods, such as the Egyptian, when symbolic concerns were also equal to aesthetic ones.

30 Monta Mozuna, Zen Temple, Eisho-Ji, Tokyo, 1979. The four-square primitive hut of Laugier is used, with certain erosions, to cover the sanctuary as a traditional baldachino. The scale dislocations are so intense that the reality looks like a model. Miniaturisation is often used to heighten an object's sanctity. (ph: M Fujitsuka)

31 Robert Mangurian and Craig Hodgetts (Studio Works), South Side Settlement, Columbus, Ohio, 1979–81. Wall-niche above paired columns will hold a future stairway to the balcony of the 'theatre'. A set of quick oppositions – flat/curved, tension/compression, concrete/paper – heightens the tension of this very restrained wall. (ph: R Mangurian)

32 Peter Hodgkinson and Taller Bofill, Church Sanctuary Meritxell, Andorra, 1974–80. Arches go from inside to out, from supporting to non-supporting role. The way they frame the landscape is clearly intended to borrow nature and bring it into the chapel. (ph: Serena Vergano)

33 Charles Jencks, Garagia Rotonda, Wellfleet, 1976–77. The 'rotonda' is like Palladio's villa of that name placed on a cross-axis with steps mounting to it from the four axes of the horizon, but unlike Palladio's grand gesture the curve is only one inch deep; this is just enough to indicate the absent dome. (ph: C Jencks)

Style and Quality

It would not be surprising if a sceptic were to ask at this point: 'What is the use of this Free Style Classicism if it embraces the second rate? At least the old classicism confined its exemplars to the best that was designed or built in the past.' This argument is not without its force, but a few things may be said to clarify, if not justify, the situation today. In all current traditions of architecture there has been a general decline in quality which has been discussed also in other areas of culture and everyday life. Our era is not distinguished for the high quality of its Modernism, Post-Modernism or Late-Modernism and this is partly caused by the variety of contending styles and philosophies. Where pluralism reigns so does confusion and a lowering of standards; where canons are commonly held and enforced, there 'perfection and beauty', two perennial concerns of older classicisms, can be aimed at if not achieved. The reason, in architecture, is not hard to guess. Only by piecemeal modifications of design models made by builder, craftsman, client and architect can anything so complex as a building be brought to a state of harmonious resolution.

Since artists and craftsmen are excluded from present building, or when included they turn out to have differing tastes and skills, no developed work is very likely. Clearly any 'high period' of architecture demands the training of a building team in a whole set of conventions that are commonly known. Christopher Wren built up such a team just as Bramante inherited, or as Giuliano Romano constituted. Excellence depends on traditions, quality on a shared style – where is the tradition and style that are commonly understood by a building team?

If one looks through the buildings in this issue, or *Post-Modern Classicism* or *Speaking a New Classicism*, one is not overwhelmed by the sensitivity or discrimination of the final products. This could be said as much of the Straight Revivalists – Terry, Greenberg, Blatteau – as of the others. If one were to publish only those designs and buildings of admitted quality, admitted by a consensus of the architects themselves, then what buildings would emerge? One by

Hans Hollein, another by Michael Graves? Would Rossi, Moore, Venturi be seen as too sectarian or not involved with the whole issue of quality? Indeed faults can be found with every building designed in the emerging Free Style Classical tradition, partly because it is so young, partly because all architecture has faults. (Those of the Pantheon have been commented on *and* overlooked for generations). A new tradition is just being constituted and 'art' (if not yet artists) is again being conceived as an integral part of it.

If we briefly review the history of this tradition we can see how tenuous it is. In the early Sixties Philip Johnson incorporated classical forms in his colonnaded buildings – the Sheldon Memorial Art Gallery (1960–63), Amon Carter Museum (1961), Follee (1962) and Lincoln Center scheme (1957–66). The white, hard-edge classicism was almost as reductive as the International Style: no real integration of art and symbolism, no deep cultural invention, no great urban idea, nothing much beyond a well-groomed travertine was attempted. Ignazio Gardella's simultaneous creations in a related style also lacked that inclusiveness which we have characterised as the essence of classicism. If this is true of Johnson's and Gardella's work then it is even more true of what could be called the

34 Robert Krier, Ritterstrasse Figure, 1980. Like Le Corbusier's monument to Vaillant Couturier, 1937, this personification mixes abstraction and figuration. Again Krier is pointing up the parallels between ancient, ruined figures, dancing nereids and modernist techniques – (ph: G Blomeyer)
35 Robert Krier, Ritterstrasse Apartments, Berlin-Kreuzberg, 1977–80. The U-shape block defines the centre of the larger city block and allows movement under the centre, flattened arch. An ordering at once reminiscent of the 1920s and Renaissance palazzo defines the common ground between these usually opposed periods of architecture. (ph: G Blomeyer)
36 Michael Graves, Referential Sketches, 1981. Graves actually spent time in a library studying Mexican, Guatamalan and Indian sources which he feels are inherent in the Spanish Mission tradition. Walls, volume, pyramid and nature set the themes.
37 Michael Graves, Public Library, San Juan Capistrano, 1981-. Various archetypes and images are woven together in a masterful synthesis which transforms the sources. Although the influence of Krier, Rossi and Kupper may be discerned it is totally absorbed, as are the local references to the Spanish Mission and vernacular style. The remnant of a gable accentuates a main window. Light hoods carry on an ordered dialogue.

34
36

35
37

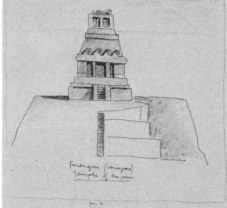

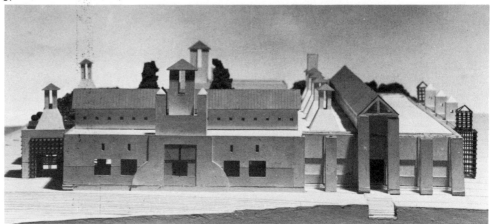

'classical-kitsch' of Minoru Yamasaki and others. The fundamentalist classicism of Louis Kahn, his Trenton Bath Houses and Bryn Mawr Dormitories, avoided this bathos and it helped keep a door open to a wider approach, but it still did not provide a place for art, convention, ornament, polychromy or our litany of elements without which a building is not fully classical.

Slowly, tentatively, one by one, elements began to reappear: by the late Sixties Venturi and then Stern brought back ornament and symbolism. By the early Seventies James Stirling, Leon Krier and Aldo Rossi reasserted the importance of a fundamental order and urbane order (but still kept shy of the full classical repertoire). Drawing shows: the Museum of Modern Art on that of the Ecole des Beaux-Arts (1975), two in New York (1977), and a series of books on the subject did a little to bring back polychromy and ornament by the late Seventies. But still, given all these influences and more, a wide synthetic tradition has hardly started to exist. Were one to ask in 1979 for the monument to Post-Modernism I would answer Charles Moore's Piazza d'Italia; in 1980 Michael Graves' Portland Pubic Services Building.[19] Of course Modernists did not admit the monument as a valid type (while they surreptitiously translated housing into monuments), but my point is a different one: our best buildings do not compare particularly well with Chartres, St Peter's, or the Sagrada Familia, or to come down a notch, the Paris Opera, or Philip Webb's little Red House. To raise such comparisons, and after all the best architecture is the judge of all architecture, might lead one to the conclusion that Free Style Classicism is closer to the primitiveness of a tradition such as the Romanesque than it is to a developed one such as Mannerism. To summarise this present state of the (undeveloped) art we might look at two of the better schemes.

Robert Krier's infill block in Berlin, analysed more fully later, has a classical palazzo U-shape plan (**34**). In appearance we can immediately see the Post-Modern hybrid sources: one-half Le Corbusier's flat white architecture of the Twenties; one-half a Renaissance ordering into base, attic and symmetrical end pavilions. Conceptually the flat white plan forms the datum from which windows recede or figural elements protrude, and in this it is more similar to the Renaissance than Modern facade. The white plane acts like Alberti's 'ordered' facades as a steady background reference for variations – here in colour, material and content. The most surprising of the last mentioned is the partly ruined figure, a pre-eroded sculpture that reminds one, variously, of the Victory of Samothrace, K F Schinkel with his flowing cape (a favourite Krier icon), a bullfighter making a rather awkward pass, a phallus surmounting a central column and, above all, the Baroque caryatids that often announce entry and the presence of the human realm in architecture (**35**). Here the *erosion* we have noted before works in a very different way to make references ambiguous and meaning primitive. If one asks what is the public meaning of this most public of gestures then we receive a semi-private answer: it's a Surrealist hulk waiting, like Man Ray's *The Enigma of Isadore Ducasse*, to declare itself. That it is a male body no one will dispute. But its precise iconographical meaning remains, and is intended to remain, unarticulated. We might say it represents the idea of anthropocentrism reaffirmed in the centre of architecture: the return of the missing body.

All this is welcome for giving the conventional meanings of caryatids – scale, identity, an empathetic response to inert material – but we can't say the sculpture is very refined or distinctive. It's one of a number of first steps (Graves' Portlandia is another) on the road to a fuller personification in architecture.

Michael Graves' San Juan Capistrano Library Scheme, which won a competition in February 1981, is another excellent design which is heading towards a more complete classicism. The primitiveness in design is evidently not just a matter of the building being at the model stage. It is sought by Graves, as in the designs which have influenced it: those by Aldo Rossi, Leon Krier and Eugene Kupper. Small, square clerestory windows of the first floor, wooden trusses of the second, and extruded pitched roof of the third are combined with the heavy curves meant to recall the nearby Spanish Mission. Other historicist references include the massive pyramidal constructions of South America (which Graves feels relate to the Spanish Mission Style) and the garden pergolas, which filter light in so many traditional cultures. So the scheme relates at once to the

primitiveness of European design and to the local context (**36, 37**).

Red pantiles, cream stucco, grey earth are not exactly the colours of San Juan Capistrano's architecture, but they are close, just as the pyramidal sun towers are a near relative. More direct are the quotations in stencilled wood and the massive columnar order taken up on one side of the courtyard. Red Bougainvillia will overflow heavy masonry walls, as it does in this locale, and water will focus the outdoor view, as is also customary here. One of the contributions that Graves brings to this tradition, with which he obviously feels sympathy, is the subtle blending of architectural and natural orders so that they intersect in an amusing way: one will erode and march into the other destroying the hard edge usual to classicism.

In sum these two designs represent high points of Post-Modern Classicism but they show how far the tradition has yet to travel before that quality is reached which can only be the result of a long, continuous search. Ornament, sculpture, convention and symbolism all remain rudimentary, at the first stage, but both Krier and Graves, as artists committed to the public realm, will no doubt push things further. Perhaps more architects will become artists, and artists will be invited back to the building site. The way ahead lies with a full integration of the *means* of architecture which classical periods have achieved in the past, and non-classical designers such as Antonio Gaudi have realised. These, especially the conventionalised periods, remain the standard and perhaps if patrons, developers and critics demanded such a standard a wider tradition would grow.

Notes

1   See John Summerson, *The Classical Language of Architecture*, Thames and Hudson, London (1980), pp 7, 8, 9. The first edition of 1963 originated as a BBC series of talks and Sir John told me the whole idea for the book stemmed from lectures intended to inform students not acquainted with classicism.
2   *Speaking a New Classicism: American Architecture Now*, with essays by Guest Curator Helen Searing and Henry Hope Reed, Smith College Museum of Art, Northampton, Mass (1981), p 9.
3   *Ibid*, pp 23, 25.
4   *Op Cit* note 1) Summerson, p 9.
5   *Ibid*, p 120, 121.
6   *Ibid*, p 9.
7   Demetri Porphyrios presented a paper at a symposium held at *Architectural Design* in December 1980 which will appear in another form in a forthcoming issue of *AD*. Others who contributed included Quinlan Terry, John Onians and Fernando Montes.
8   Gavin Stamp, 'The Master Builder', *Spectator*, 7 Feb 1981, pp 24–5. 'But they do not look so much at Renaissance Classicism – that would be too difficult and demanding – but rather at the austere, abstracted geometry of Neo-Classicism, which is both easier to do and also satisfies the latent megalomania of architects.'
9   See the entry 'Classics' in *Encyclopedia Britannica*, 11th edition, 1910–11, Vol 5–6, p 448. The article points out that English usage is in accordance with this. The earliest usage of 'classical' is the phrase 'classical and canonical' found in *Europae Speculum* of Sir Edwin Sandys, 1599. Joseph Rykwert discusses these sources and shows that the word *classicus* also derives from *calare*, 'to call'; but by the late republic the term was reserved for members of the richest class. See Joseph Rykwert, *The First Moderns*, The Architects of the Eighteenth Century, The MIT Press, Cambridge and London (1980), pp 1–3, 20, 21.
10 Norris Kelly Smith, *Frank Lloyd Wright*, A Study in Architectural Content, Prentice Hall, Englewood, New Jersey (1966), p 42. (Note)
11 Nicholas Penny, 'Cross Purposes', *Times Literary Supplement*, 3 April, 1981, p 383.
12 Arthur O Lovejoy, 'The Discrimination of Romanticisms', *Publications of the Modern Language Association*, XXXIX (1924), p 232.
13 'It was William W Gunn, in 1819, who published his *Inquiry into the Origin and Influence of Gothic Architecture* in the *Quarterly Review*, and there explicitly defended the choice of the term Romanesque as indicating corrupted Roman. The Italian termination -esco, he thought, had precisely this connotation.' See E H Gombrich *Norm and Form*, Studies in the Art of the Renaissance, Phaidon Press, London, 1966, p 85. I have found this essay immensely suggestive as subsequent notes will reveal.
14 Certain English critics such as Kenneth Frampton and several Italian Marxist critics deplore the way architectural imagery is purveyed, then 'consumed' and 'regurgitated' without understanding. In many cases their censure may be justified, but they often miss those crucial cases when the architect *does* manage to transform his source material.
15 For numerical taxonomy see the *Scientific American* article on the subject, Dec 1966; for my use of it in architecture see 'Pigeon-holing made difficult', in *AD* (Nov 1969), p 582, and *Modern Movements in Architecture*, Penguin Books (Harmondsworth 1973), p 188.
16 See E H Gombrich above (note 13). *Norm and Form*, pp 94–5, and his essay 'Raphael's "Madonna della Sedia"', *op cit*, pp 64–80.
17 E H Gombrich also argues that norms, or ideas, have to be brought into a discussion of formal values. *Ibid*, pp 81–99.
18 *Ibid*, pp 83–6.
19 As far as I could see then these were the two built urban projects that summarised the most strands of classicism at that time; hence my new chapter and introduction to the third edition of *The Language of Post-Modern Architecture*, written in 1980.

Charles Moore
Schinkel's Free Style Pavilion
and the Berlin Tegeler Hafen Scheme

Since primitive times, and especially in eras of turmoil and trouble, people have found solace in the ritual repetition of set phrases, the magic incantation of proven formulae. It is never very clear to the unbeliever just where the proof of the proven came from, how efficacious the rain dance is at bringing on the rain, but the dancers brook no falterings of the faith. For most of the history of the world as well, and especially in times that seem more supportive, people have made the world their own by exploring it, discovering it, and especially by transforming it, turning the old into new. Sometimes in a revolutionary way that overthrows the old (as in the years about 1910), sometimes in a way that honours it while it makes something else (as in the years flanking 1500).

Architecture of course exhibits both forms of behaviour, the ritual orthodox and the (more or less) free style, and these days we seem to have our choice. For some of us, the only way to inhabit the world is to transform it, to make it our own, and we can look for special support to what I'll call the generation of 1810 – architects like Karl Friedrich Schinkel in Prussia, Sir John Soane in England and Thomas Jefferson in Virginia. All of them were moving with vigorous enthusiasm into a new age of industry and (for some) democracy; but all felt buttressed by the classical past, from which their modern arrangements were seen to derive.

A splendid example of this classical free style is Karl Friedrich Schinkel's Pavilion at the Charlottenburg Palace, in Berlin. It is mostly a simple rectangular solid, pure enough for Le Corbusier himself; on the upper floor it has a pair of simplified pilasters on each side, to flank and therefore describe porches. Just above the pilasters, all around the building runs a thin incision; almost invisible but all-powerful, the cut of the Zen archer, a whispered delimitation of shaft from classical entablature, an invocation without orthodoxy of a hallowed past.

A much more massive addition to the pavilion is a balcony all the way around, just below its waist, its simple shapes all made of iron – about as modern an intervention as could be imagined, though its underside is painted blue and with stars. Confident and eclectic, this work embraces the old, while it transforms it into the new. No orthodoxy could match it, no formula could recreate it, but it gives solace and support while we try to ring transformations of our own.

Charles Moore

1 Schinkel pavilion, Schlosspark, Charlottenburg, 1824–25. *The first time I went to Berlin James Stirling told me to be sure to see Schinkel's Pavilion; one of the things that delighted me most about it was the way that a bay, shaft and entablature are made. The shaft is distinguished from the entablature, or upper fifth of the building, by a single, thin incised line just above the capitals that is almost invisible, especially in photographs. That deft, light touch, the slice of the archaism with a latter-day rapier, this real transformation means more to me than all the earnest apings of classical forms.* (CM)
2 Tegeler Hafen, perspective of cultural centre plaza looking south along Karolinenstrasse. *What I was very excited about when we were designing the cultural center of our Berlin scheme was the ambiguous zone between the self-satisfied, formal and classical buildings and the warehouses along the edge of the water. Trondheim comes to mind as a city which has a batch of big rectangular buildings bangety-bang along the edge of the commercial-industrial waterway with the mixed image of being right at the edge of one thing and another. One thing that gave a considerable push to our ambiguity, and the picture we looked at by far the most, was Schinkel's Römischer Bäder at Potsdam which is a bunch of classical shapes disposed of in a picturesque way which are then sliced off at the top by a flat trellis which cuts off the sky from a set of levels underneath and our insertion of the warehouse image was meant to accomplish the same end.* (CM)

1
2

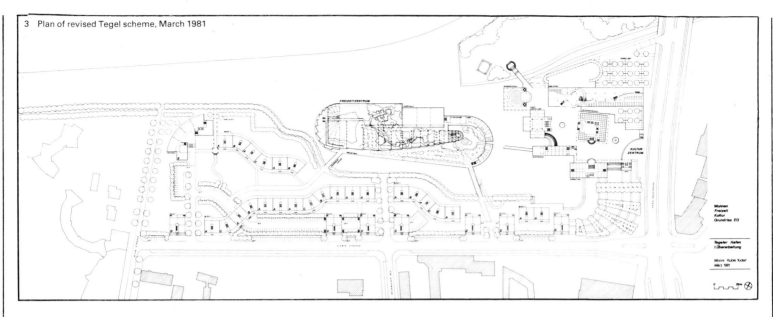

3 Plan of revised Tegel scheme, March 1981

Moore Ruble Yudell, Tegel Harbour Competition, Berlin 1980
Project Team: Charles Moore, John Ruble, Robert Yudell. Colour: Tina Beebe

This invitational design competition focuses the efforts of city agencies, private developers, and an international cast of architects to organise planning for one of West Berlin's most attractive recreational areas. Tegel Harbour was developed for industry, and connects a delightful surburban village with a chain of lakes and canals, as well as forested open space, which provide Berliners with week-end outings, seemingly far from the city centre. The competition programme called for residential, cultural, and sports facilities, aimed at the conversion of the harbour from industrial to re-

creational uses. Our general plan for the site makes water the connecting theme, with each of the programme elements relating to the water's presence in some special way.

The cultural centre almost has the feeling of a converted warehouse district on the water front, but with a classical organisation, lightness of detail, and colour reminiscent of K F Schinkel, one of Berlin's best-loved architects of the 19th century. A large library is included in the centre facilities. Our design for the library creates a generous, well lighted reading room, through which passes a dramatic wall of bookshelves, with a gallery for access to the upper level. Large triple-hung windows allow access to a reading terrace in good weather, and occasional views to an adjacent park all year round.
Charles Moore

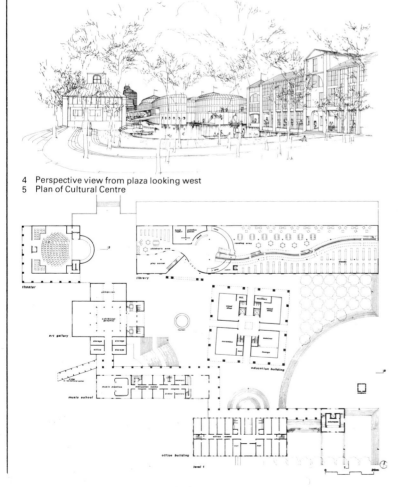

4 Perspective view from plaza looking west
5 Plan of Cultural Centre

6 Adult Library, perspective looking east
7 Perspective view looking north-east across plaza

Oswald Mathias Ungers
Five Lessons from Schinkel
and the Architecture Museum in Frankfurt

'Many are trained in criticism, but few in the art of making. Therefore, mastery must be respected.' (Karl Friedrich Schinkel).

There shall certainly be many who will subsequently give their opinions on Schinkel, but shall they also recognise his mastery and draw lessons from his 'making'?

Objectively, from the point of view of the history of architecture, Schinkel's position as 'the German architect par excellence' has long been secure and was documented more than once to the disadvantage of the cause. What remains to be said, in most cases, today, is frequently nothing but smug presentation and melodramatic exercises to the life and work of the great architect. For it has long gotten about: Schinkel is 'in' and that not only in this country, but also out there. Even the Japanese try to put themselves into the humanistic world of Neoclassical antiquity and are meditating on an architecture à la Schinkel: Schinkel is suddenly *en vogue*. After that long and arid path of formal celibacy, his architectural vocabulary is institutionalised. He is party-talk between New York and Tokyo and fills the young architects' heads and portfolios. His work is inexhaustible material for lectures and the magic formula of academia. One wears Schinkel, feels acknowledged and is walking on solid ground. The 'new tendency' has finally found its patron saint and stylite.

The style is right. It can be excellently described, imitated, changed, quoted and carried on. The spectre of the master is so complex, that anyone may avail himself freely of it be he a romanticist or inclined toward classicism, a technologist or architect of the old style, conscious of his craftsmanship, an incorrigible functionalist or a profound mind that sets signs. They all fit under the wide cloak of the 'man for all seasons'. With him they all find their place. He is at home in all styles, techniques and methods and masters all principles simultaneously.

But this is the point at which irony turns upon itself. Subjectively seen, Schinkel is neither stylite nor monument, neither secured nor institutionalised. Quite to the contrary, he is as controversial and alive as ever. Provided, of course, one does not fall for the seductive usage of his diverse forms of style, but is ready to draw general lessons from both his ideas and the concept carrying them.

For Schinkel's ideas are independent of the climate of opinion and transcend temporal conditions. They pertain to the fundamental principles of architecture. Who, with the exception of some polemicising critics, can still be interested in discussing Schinkel's genius or such architectural questions as antiquity versus gothic, classicism versus romanticism, organic versus rational expression, form versus function, democratic building versus monumental architecture, progressive or historical building? As though there was anything left to be said about the complexity of building and, above all, about the phenomenon of Schinkel, if one exhausts oneself in antitheses.

If there is a lesson to be learnt from Schinkel's work, then it is precisely that of the unity of the opposites. It is the teaching of the *coincidentia oppositorum* originated by Nikolaus Cusanus in opposition to the dogmatism of the Middle Ages at the threshold to the Englightenment and at the onset of a spiritual renewal. This concept, that denotes the unification of the opposites to form a whole, is the true intellectual background of Schinkel's work. It is not the harmony of the classical style in contrast to the spiritualisation of the gothic expression, not the symmetrical austerity in contrast to relativised order, but the mutual conditioning of classicism and romanticism, of order and coincidence, of absolute

austerity and complete freedom. It is the 'coincidence of the opposites' and not their isolation that results in the complete, the living Gestalt. Ideologisation of concepts does not create the unity of the whole, but is created by their intellectual dependency and conditioning. The dialectical principle is the true formative principle of Schinkel's work, which consititutes the first lesson to be drawn from it. It is the intellectual unity of the things in their formal diversity.

This unity of things is based on two presuppositions: on the continuity of history on the one hand, and on the continuity of ideas on the other hand. For Schinkel, architecture was not a historical sequence of styles ranging from antiquity to gothic,modernism and further on to post-modernism and post-post-modernism and so on. For Schinkel and his contemporaries history was both the history of ideas and their gradual development in thesis and antithesis up to the highest degree of perfection. This is the reason why Schinkel's work does not fit within any one self-contained category of style, but goes on from station to station, from one position to the next, in its evolution and perfection of architectural ideas. Style means nothing. It is merely ornament, subsequently put on and added. It is interchangeable, conditioned by time and ephemeral. The idea is everything. It is abiding. And that constitutes the second lesson from Schinkel's intellectual legacy. It is both an insight into the things and realisation of the fundamental principle underlying formation. Without this principle, without the idea, without theme and spiritual concept, architecture touches but the surface and loses itself in the formal ornament. Then, it is merely appliqué work, *aperçu*, historical quote and if worse comes to worse, a joke.

But it is the idea that keeps a building alive beyond the different trends and fads. It cannot become antiquated, fall out of fashion, but remains fresh and new as at the hour at which it was born. Its clarity outlasts political abuse and defies corruption by either an individual or systems.

Any building that is not theme unto itself is, intellectually seen, a triviality. Of course it may fulfil necessary purposes and needs and also meet justified technological demands, but if it does not transcend the mere fulfilment of purposes and presents itself as idea, too, then it defies architecture's claim to be an expression of mental universality and simply remains a banality. In any case, Schinkel's architecture was not only concerned with the fulfilment of needs, but first and foremost with the universality of thought.

An architecture that forgoes this claim, moving about exclusively in what is commonplace, must of necessity put on a technical strait jacket and will finally get caught up in chaos. An intellectual concept, however, is capable of change. It is flexible and adapts itself to the respective conditions of place and time. This constitutes the third lesson that is transmitted to us through Schinkel's work. It is the teaching of the transformation of the things, of what has gone into what is to come, of what is into what is new, of the past into the future. It is that transformation that changes what exists by means of morphological transformation.

Architecture is just like nature. It, too, is capable of changing from one Gestalt into another. These forms are never self-contained, but invariably contain their opposite too. What is meant here is the process of formation and transformation of thoughts, demands, objects and conditions, from one state into another. In reality, this implies that the process of thinking takes place in qualitative values and not in quantitative facts. A process, then, that is based on synthesis rather than on analysis. Yet this must not be taken to mean that analytical thought is superfluous, but rather that analysis

1–5 Photographs of Schinkel's Glienecke, by O M Ungers

and synthesis alternate as naturally as inhalation and exhalation, quoting Goethe.

Just as the meaning of a whole sentence differs from that of a sum of individual words, so the creative thought is the characteristic unit with which to take in a series of facts and not only to analyse them as something that is composed of individual parts. The awareness that reality can be grasped through imagination constitutes the true creative process, because it creates a higher degree of order than the simple method of testing, examining and controlling. All physical phenomena are forms in their metamorphosis from one state into another. This thinking in morphological transformation constitutes the transition from thinking in metrical space to that in the visionary space of coherent systems, from concepts of the same nature to those of diverse form.

This principle of morphological transformation is the true formative principle in Schinkel's work. It creates concepts that go beyond the historical meaning. They endure as creative principle. For this reason, Schinkel did not think of replacing the 'old' by the 'new'. He felt that it was his task to continue and to complement what existed. He wished to complete what had already been begun and to discover the physiognomy and poetry of the place. It was the quest of the idea of Berlin that caused Schinkel not to replace the old Berlin by a new one, as was attempted by later generations time and again up to Hilbersheimer who proposed the total city and similar such endeavours only with different formal means. Schinkel was searching for the identity of the city and not for the formal principle. He wanted to transform the face that existed in perhaps its fundamental outlines into another one, to discover the existing traces and continue them. It was his endeavour to perpetuate the language of the place, to carry out a dialogue with the given and to recognise the *genius loci*.

However, this also implies acceptance of the past, but even more the presence of history. It is not negation of the significance of historical events, nor is it their rejection out of misunderstood progress. And this constitutes the fourth lesson transmitted by Schinkel's work. It is the teaching of history as a living tradition. If historical thought is missing, there can be no thought of an architecture for the place for which it is created. It receives its life from the place that has a past. An architecture that renounces historical reference remains abstract and theoretical, it will never be meaningful and alive. Historical tradition contains the roots of a new formation and it is this humanistic consciousness that constitutes the creative cause for the origination of an architecture of place, nay, is exclusively due to it, as Schinkel himself states in his writings.

A new development cannot be continued unless it proceeds from both the sense and consciousness of history. Of course, this presupposes that history is not perverted into a receptacle of forms and styles from which to draw as one's fancy would have it. It would be a travesty of history, at best, if its products were to be recorded in a catalogue of clichés and stereotypical examples. If we wish to obtain from history, then this can only mean that we realise the metaphysical values and fundamental principles underlying external appearances. History is not a cook book of ready-made recipes, but an encyclopaedical dictionary of the development of the human mind. This dictionary contains the vocabulary of the creative confrontation with reality. However, it also contains the key to the challenges of today's tasks.

An architecture that wants to forgo this mental storehouse cannot itself be the carrier of intellectual values. Any creative architecture is tied into a historical continuum from which it receives its true designation. Consciousness of this temporal continuum constitutes the fundamental realisation of humanism. It was this humanistic consciousness that has enabled us to see things in their mental interconnectedness and not in their dogmatic isolation. For this reason any dogmatic architecture is inimical to history, for it derives its existence from the claim to exclusivity inherent in its own dogmas. It does not matter whether it concerns so-called 'Modern Architecture', the architecture of Absolutism or a dogmatised popular one. In their exclusivity they all understand themselves as the sole beatific teaching. Any historically oriented architecture, however, is open and adaptable, since it recognises relativisation as principle.

The principle of exclusivity also accounts for the fact that an architecture that is based on a dogma is puristic, one-dimensional and anti-life. Historical architecture, on the other hand, is rich, controversial and close to life. It is complex and all-comprehensive. It connects where the dogma separates. It correlates realities where the dogma isolates. It seeks the unity of the parts of a composition while the dogma is dealing only with the part itself and its systematisation. Historical architecture seeks Gestalt, the dogmatic one seeks function.

Finally, this is the fifth lesson of Schinkel. It is the teaching of the unity in diversity which is concerned with the unity of nature and culture, of the grown and the built, of environment and architecture. Schinkel's designs and buildings are not only part of the mental world of ideas, but also amalgamate the organic world of nature. They are not conceived in contrast to their natural surroundings. They do not wish to assert themselves against the landscape in which they stand, nor do they fight it. Instead of separating from nature they unite with it to form a morphological whole, so that they become a part of nature, just as nature becomes a part of the built. Here, the concept of the unification of the opposite shows forth, once more, in an indescribable intensification. It presents itself in an enrichment which achieves an utmost fulfilment of harmonic thought, in which are revealed the highest moments of happiness in art.

Just as, in a slow process of gradual liberation, the cave transformed itself into the stone structure and finally into the perfect case of the Parthenon, so Schinkel's architecture reflects the stages of this development. It embraces the entire spectrum ranging from the archaic to the perfected. It is nature and culture, cave and filigree, stone and scaffolding, wall and lattice, earth and air, containment and dissolution, matter and mind at the same time. It unifies the extremes in the concept of morphology which embrace all stages, the highest as well as the lowest, dream as well as reality, form as well as presentiment. This is perhaps Schinkel's most profound secret and at the same time his most beautiful and valuable legacy.

O M Ungers
(Translated by Johanna Goehner)

The Architectural Museum, Frankfurt

The site for the architectural museum lies on the Schaumain embankment in Frankfurt. The museum forms part of an overall development scheme which has become known in Frankfurt as 'The Museum Bank'. Under this scheme a row of museums has been proposed, which will partly make use of existing buildings along the Schaumain embankment. The Museum Bank scheme pursues several noteworthy aims. Firstly, it plans to create a new cultural centre for the city. It is reviving the old humanist idea of a spiritual and cultural forum for a city, as first realised in the museum island of Berlin in the 19th century. Secondly, the scheme creates new and suitable functions for the existing buildings on the bank of the Main, thereby retaining an architecture historically associated with the area. Thirdly, the scheme puts into practice the idea of a decentralisation of functions, which makes the idea of an amalgamation of functions, culture, serviceability, business and housing feasible, both in particular and in general.

These three goals should not be underestimated: they represent starting points for a modern urban development, and their significance extends far beyond the actual local context. They show a tendency which is of great import for contemporary urban development, wherever the site may be. The details of the museum building and the outlines of the scheme should also be understood in terms of these assumptions. Within the framework of this urban scheme, the architectural museum was allotted a double villa on a relatively small plot of land on the corner of the Schaumainkai and Schweizerstrasse. The villa itself is hardly of any historical value architecturally. Although externally it resembles the architecture of the Bibliotheca Laurentiana, it is only with a certain feeling of irony that one remembers the great prototype. That, however, is not the point.

It is the sentimental value of the house which matters. The house has become part of people's collective memory and this has left its mark on the site and the history of the place. This value justifies its preservation. Of course it would be simpler and, objectively speaking, also better to build a new museum. It would even be cheaper. However, the value of the place justifies the decision to preserve the house and to include it in a new museum scheme.

There are two possibilities regarding the preservation: either the building can be restored to what it was, or the old substance can be incorporated into a new scheme, in which it becomes the content and subject of the scheme. The first proposition was already eliminated on functional grounds: the houses were not suitable for museum purposes. The second possibility thus remained, namely to improve the old building and turn it into a museum. Now how did this happen? Firstly, the entire plot of land was turned into a house or interior by building a wall around it. By doing this the old house itself became an object or exhibit in an exhibition area, whilst being at the same time a place where exhibitions would be held. The house thus takes on a significance which goes far beyond its proper, original purpose. As an object it is distanced.

The ceiling loads did not comply with the building regulations, so the house had to be gutted. Only the external shell was preserved. A new construction is placed within the now empty building and this structure takes on the new exhibition functions. The lighting of the rooms comes from an additional lightwell built into the centre of the house.

The architectural theme that ensues from this is therefore that of the 'house within a house'. The outer layer is a thick wall containing niches, recesses and hollow spaces. It can be compared with a city wall. The next layer consists of an outlined wall with windows, pillars, pilasters, sections and fillets, which stands within the outer wall. Within this in turn there is a framework formed as a type of scaffold or trellis. Lastly there is a room boundary, which consists of a tracery and is glazed.

One room thus stands within another: an outer layer of wall, an inner wall, a trellis and, as the peak of refinement, the tracery, in succession. This morphological succession of areas of space from the outside leading inwards represents the actual spatial schema and becomes the architectonic theme of the museum. The outer wall is built of heavy stone, the outlined wall of plaster and stone, the trellis of concrete and the three-dimensional tracery in steel and glass. The form thus corresponds with the content and the function. The only new elements visible from the outside are the outer layer of wall and the inner tracery, which protrudes above the roof level of the old house.

The morphological concept behind the design also includes the metamorphosis of space, in the sense of an infinite continuity of inner and outer rooms. The 'room within a room' principle enables the visitor to walk from an outer room into an inner room, which is then itself an outer room in relation to the next inner room, and so on. It is a sequence without end and thus expresses real as well as abstract continuity. The continuity of space itself is the principle behind the construction, and both the functions and the local conditions comply with this principle. It is a principle based on the amalgamation of contrasting features, rather than on their separation.

It is based on the Coincidentia Oppositorum, as coined by Nikolaus von Kues, that is, on the concurring of antitheses which have a reciprocal conditioning effect on each other, rather than excluding each other. It is in this light that the inner court should be understood. It consists of a perfect trellised room, from which the existing chestnut tree breaks through.

This is once again an exaggerated statement on the application of the construction principle: the abstract cage is contrasted with the natural object, the tree. It symbolises the contrasting of rationalised with natural space, and the restrictedness and the unity of these two anthitheses within their morphological dependency. The architectonic concept is also a paradigm for the city. It should be seen as a spatial microcosm within the microcosmic sphere of the city.

O M Ungers
(Translated from the original German by Angela Wilkes)

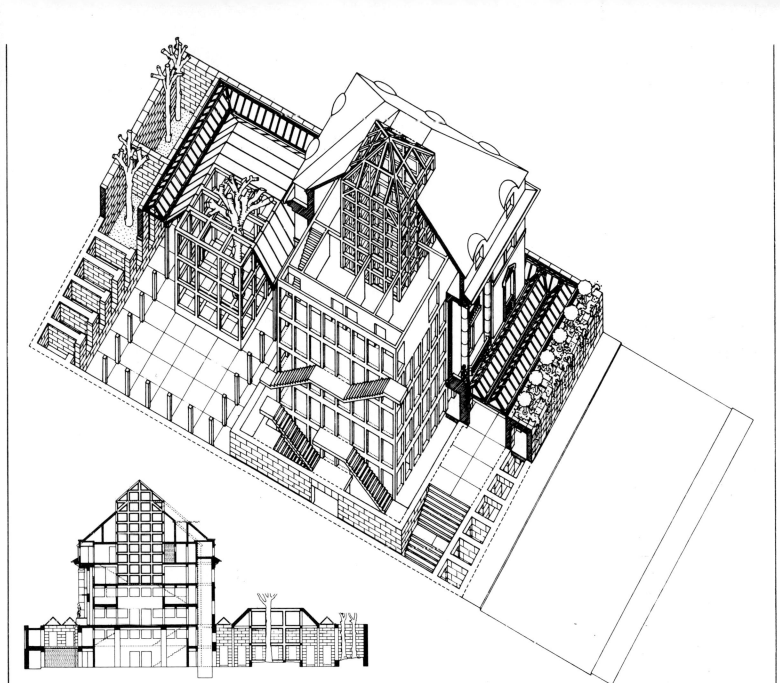

Axonometric, section and level plans 2, 3, 4 and 5

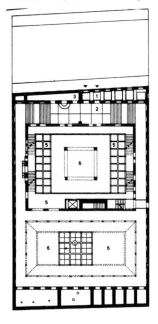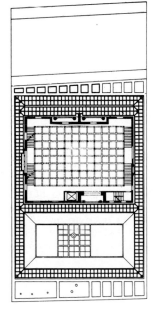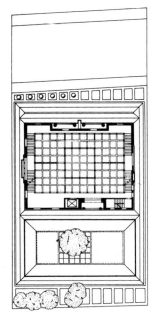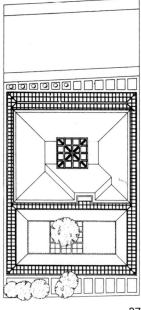

Arata Isozaki

The Ledoux Connection

Ledoux, during my graduate days in the early 1950s, was one of my heroes. At that time it was difficult to obtain material about his work in Japan, and we could only surmise the content from illustrations in magazines or art-books. I remember the strong impression that I received from Hans Sedlemeyer's book *Verlust der Mitte* in which he begins with a description from Ledoux's Maison des Gardes Agricoles.

Towards the end of the 1950s much discussion and argument occurred around me which later resulted in Metabolism. This acrobatic unification of the Buddhist concept of *Samsāra*, metempsychosis (the transmigration of souls), with technology was really attractive at the time, but I was not satisfied because it was connected to a temporary fragile expression as seen in the traditional architecture of Japan. Rather I felt a far greater interest in the composition of massive, three-dimensional Platonic solids which is absent in the Japanese tradition. This was in fact in direct opposition to the general trend of Japanese Modern architects at that time who were attempting to discover Modernism in the spatial composition of the traditional architecture of Japan. It was the lack of refinement in Ledoux's work which appealed to me as a far closer model to the original form.

At that time my interest concerned the fantasy in his work. I tried to interpret and elucidate in relation to Utopia and attempted to explain why he produced the plan of Cité Ideal. However, I could not understand the originality of his design. During the Metabolist era, most of us competed in the contrivance of producing plans for the future city and I inferred that he must be one of the visionary urban designers. It is only after some experiences of design that I came to appreciate the originality and uniqueness of his work. From the middle of the 1960s I designed several independent houses, each being based upon Platonic solids. Thus I combined the form of cube, sphere, cylinder, etc, to make each house. One day while I was cataloguing the realised schemes and drawings I suddenly noticed that they bore a resemblance to Maison de Campagne, included in the Cité Ideal. I did not remember referring to Ledoux during the design of any of these houses. Rather I remembered that I had devoted myself solely to the pursuit of the manipulation of the abstract geometric solid. In this process I gradually increased the variations of these houses and then found that they had become closer to the Maison de Campagne series.

When Ledoux produced his plans he must have carried out quite the same manipulations as I did, an idea that occurred to me when I saw the result of my house designs. I had unconsciously 'run after his method'. The discovery of this resemblance urged me to realise two things: that I had seized the clue to his design process, and that I could re-read my own work through comparing it with Ledoux's.

Compared with his contemporaries', Ledoux's work contains many deviations, exaggerations and deformations. They differ from the exquisite displacement as seen in the courtyard of Giulio Romano's Palazzo del Té or from the overlapping of different and diverse patterns as seen in the facade of Palladio's Il Redentore. The free transformation of the orthodox classical models of Vitruvius was of course common to them all. Ledoux, however, put his endeavour chiefly to the free composition of the three-dimensional solid. The basic elements he adopted for use are the cube, cylinder, split pediment, triumphal arch, and serliana, each element bearing equal importance. That is to say that the compositional hierarchy which was inherent in classical architecture was disintegrated, and the element came to stand independent of its relation to other elements.

This free-style may be called Classicism or Neoclassicism, as all the elements he adopted were derived from the vocabulary of classical architecture. His manner of ordination, his syntax, however, was quite unique. This originality is revealed particularly in the Barrières of Paris and the group of Maison de Campagne, the former toll houses and the latter small independent houses. As all of them are small independent buildings, the functions are limited. In this limitation, however, he developed infinite variations. The Barrières are composed of pure solids such as the cube and cylinder, on which are attached a rusticated colonnade and lintel; sometimes a triumphal arch, seemingly out of scale, was superimposed to emphasise the massiveness. As the tollhouse was also a city gate, the dominating quality of a fortress might have been required. Anyhow here the massiveness was emphasised beyond the normal sense of balance. In the houses of Maison de Campagne in Chaux the surfaces were extremely simplified to the point of becoming totally expressionless. It brings forth the effect of raising the cylinder and cube to the surface. Here we must realise that the professions of the inhabitants – ie, woodcutter, cooper, artist and writer – become the direct theme for architectural expression. Although metaphorical, a more literal symbolism is evident. This symbolism is the reason for his work being given the name of 'narrative architecture'.

When I look back to my design of Fujimi Country Clubhouse (1975), I cannot remember having referred to Ledoux. The first intention was to float a barrel vault with a semi-cylindrical shaped section low above the ground, letting it meander. Consequently, most of the design energy was devoted to the problem of the structural and visual materialisation. We tried to develop to the utmost limit the structural form in its resistance to earthquake. Thus at the final stage, in the consideration of the canopy, I thought of it as a Serliana. Even at that point I did not recollect the idea of Ledoux's Maison des Directeurs de la Loue. Nevertheless, on its completion I felt that I had proceeded a stage closer to Ledoux. Ledoux's scheme for the water-gate directly shows in the elevation, the vacant cylindrical-shaped section which permits the passage of water, thereby symbolising the water gate.

At Fujimi it was intended that eye movement would run along the inside of the vault creating an ebb and flow of people. Water and air being similarly fluid, I presume that I must have unconsciously selected the same form of vault and in my expression of exposing its section, as Ledoux did, I must have taken the same route as Ledoux himself.

In the hotel wing of Tsukuba Civic Centre which is now under construction (to be completed in 1982), I continued my method of combining cubes of varying scales. As it is an urban scheme, rustication is applied to the base wall. As the construction site is located in a stone-quarrying district, the use of stone was naturally required. Moreover, as Tsukuba Civic Centre is a complex of this town I decided to introduce architectural motifs of urban context. Since rustication and pure geometric form are also major features of the Barrières it is natural that a remarkable resemblance to Ledoux is seen in my scheme.

Looking back on my 20 years of being attracted to the work of Ledoux, I wish, rather than to see his work from a distance, to analyse, struggle with and digest it; and to approach more directly not his superficial style but some secret of freedom which enables architecture to narrate by itself. What I am aiming at is the realisation in architecture of the fantasy expressed in his drawings.

Arata Isozaki

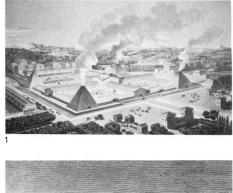

1

2

3

4

5
6

1   C N Ledoux, view of the Gun Foundry. Emil Kaufmann writes: 'This system (of independent pavilions) appears also in the Gun Foundry where the main accent has been shifted from the center to the pyramids in the corners . . . single elements do not form into pictorial *ensembles*, contrary to the Baroque complexes . . .'. Note the Free Style combination of Palladian motif and truncated pyramid and dome.

2   C N Ledoux, Lumberman's House made from horizontal courses of timber stacked in a pyramidal form and entered through a Palladian motif

3   C N Ledoux, House of the Directors of the River Loue

4   C N Ledoux, House of the Director, Chaux, 1770–80.

5   Isozaki, Hotel facade of the Tsukuba Civic Center, 1980–82. Roughly a tripartite division with heavy quoins, banded rustication, growing out of the wall stereometry and inflecting at an angle to direct movement inside (ph: T Kitajima, *Retoria*)

6   Isozaki, Tsukuba Civic Centre with a free interpretation of various classical themes: Michelangelo's Campidoglio is sunken, not raised (in the centre) and eroded by a Hollein estuary (left). A tartan grid unifies the main level while Gravesian pavilions and Rossian volumes and windows play above this. Isozaki has already done consummate variations on the Modernist's vocabulary while here his eclectic mannerism achieves a wider set of sources (ph: A Isozaki)

Hans Hollein

Haus Molag, Vienna, 1977, 1980–81

An elegant plan disciplines the volumes, as Adolf Loos would have liked. Severe symmetry on one side, like Loos' Tzara House, and rippling asymmetry on the garden side – the reverse of Loos' Steiner House. In fact the building reverses the Steiner typology which is square-faced garden versus round-faced street side.

Here the rounded roof contains a solarium which can slide apart to reveal a Viennese luxury: swimming on the rooftops. The pronounced emphasis on barrel vaults – shared by Hollein's friend Isozaki – and circles is conventionally related to solar symbolism in the classical tradition. The oculus of the Pantheon is, as it were, extruded sideways through the vault window to then turn at right angles and make a plunge into the pool. It penetrates the floor to arrive, appropriately, at the next symbolic focus, the dining room – a centrally planned church with paired columns (almost Santa Costanza) which slides, miraculously, on to a wavy open plan and garden view. A subsidiary focus is the other circle: a garden room open to the sky. From this one can proceed, at breakneck speed, down ultra-thin stairs to the garden. Stair-curve and window-tilt on this facade (see axonometrics) recall the mannerist 'limp curves' which Rem Koolhaas has done so much to publicise.

The building sits somewhat in the middle of the lot – formally on two adjacent sides and semi-informally on the other two. This disjunction may appear wilful if we expect unity, but of course there is much classical precedent for the opposition. The garden, wavy side may appear stiff – a consequence of fabricating it in straight sections – and again there is precedent for this in 1930s classicism (perhaps a deplorable one). Undeniable is the sophistication of combining usually separate frames of reference and style, all reduced within the Loosian vocabulary. Perhaps Hollein is making a regional argument here. In any case it feels like the Wittgenstein House and other local buildings, and one awaits completion expecting the usual Hollein virtuosity in detail and symbolism – which will give it life.

CJ

1   Aerial view from garden side with solarium closed. The understated eclecticism is apparent in this view. To left Italian stair, arch and open pergola; centre below is a modern Germanic window wall; top is the Roman barrel vault and Georgian window scheme.
2   Main street view with symmetrical side windows and the blank square with small square centred window – a motif Loos lent Rossi.
3   Plan of first-floor dining area. Note the paired columns surrounding the formal, small dining table versus the lonely column. A bi-axial symmetry is eaten away to one side. Part of the plan might almost be a Palladian nine-square problem.
4   Plan of the ground floor. Originally the scheme was conceived for two families.
5   Axonometric of garden side; solarium closed.
6   Axonometric of the main entrance side. Note the solarium opened up.

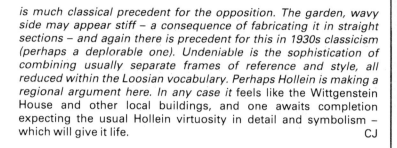

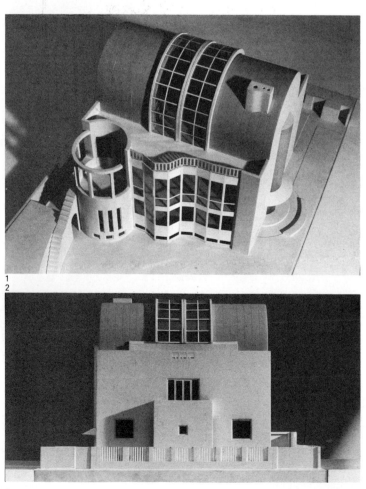

1
2

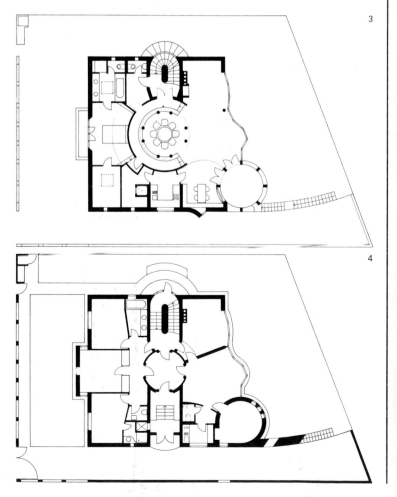

3

4

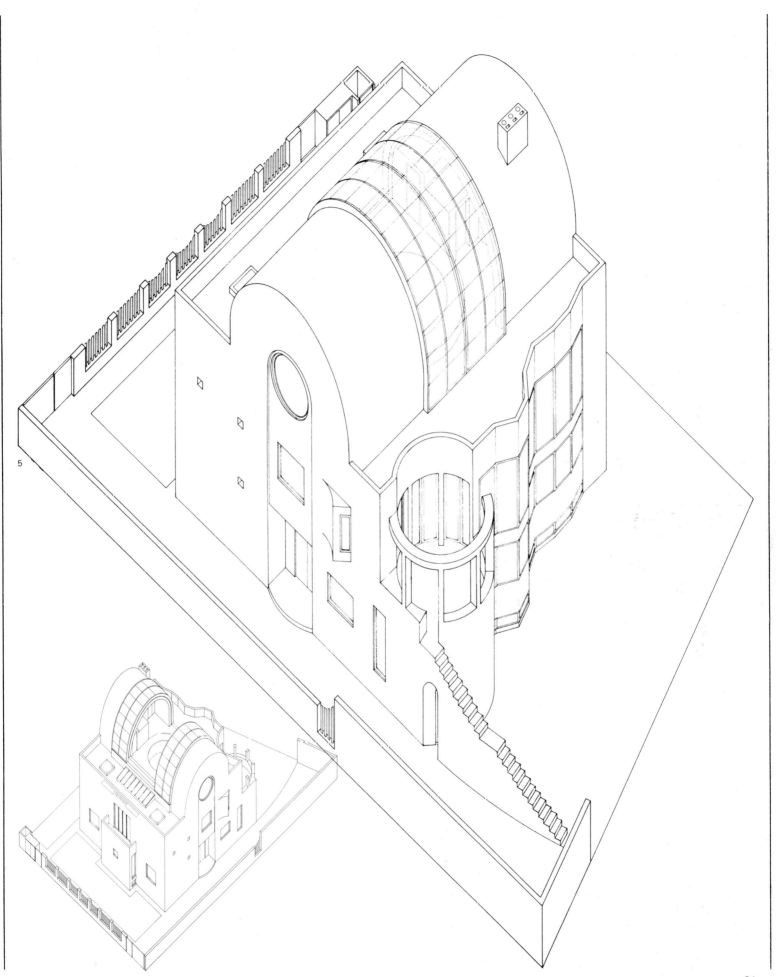

Charles Jencks
Chicago Post-Modern Classicism

Universalism between Mies and Free Style

At several periods in history Classicism, like Catholicism, has claimed to be universal. Indeed like the Modernism of Gropius and Mies van der Rohe it had (and has) grand pretensions, even imperialistic ideals, which seek to convince different cultures of its universal applicability. Hence the classical style in Greek colonies, hence the colonial classicism of India and America. A 19th-century classicist might call his style, rather pompously, 'eternal'; a theorist such as Choisy or Guadet might point to underlying archetypes (or 'elements') which all architecture has but which the classical style (especially in its 'classic' phases) makes into simple and beautiful statements; a poet such as Paul Valéry might stress the perfection achieved by the evolution of an archetype towards its inherent essence (as if there *were* some entelechy at work after all); and then a polemicist such as Le Corbusier might turn this into a theory of cultural evolution and speak of solving the 'problem of perfection' by the constant refining of a 'standard'. Somewhere in every classical revival there are these ideals driving the architects on to express the abstract, perfect and universal solution to a problem.

The individual, idiosyncratic, time-bound and regional are all suppressed. If one really believes in this universalism, he stops calling it classicism or modernism and terms it simply Architecture (with mandatory capital A). We may, afterwards, see how rooted and local these solutions are, but at the time they seem a pure, aesthetic conjunction of reason and technology.

There is another more permissive and pluralistic version of this same universalism, comparable to a regionalism within the Catholic Church. Under this Free Style interpretation the universal archetypes are also seen to exist, but there is much greater latitude in their manipulation. They may be realised in local or new materials, they may be combined with exotic styles to produce a hybrid, they may be enlarged or shrunken in scale so as to be almost unrecognisable. Indeed so great may the distortions be in Free Style Classicism that one may prefer a neologism or national appellation to the alternative of identifying the classical elements. This is the course usually adopted when historians refer to such various things as Romanesque, Viking Style or Art Deco, in spite of the fact that all three use basic classical archetypes and part of a classical vocabulary. In analysing recent Chicago architecture we will make use of the two kinds of classicism – the Canonic and Free Style, the generic and eclectic or, in the local argot of Al Capone, the straight and the crooked.

Most good Chicago architects have always been able to do both. Charles Atwood and D H Burnham could produce a reasonable, if somewhat dull, essay in academic classicism for their Hall of Fine Arts, 1893, but then stretch the language to breaking point with their Reliance Building of 1894–95. Here we may *just* speak of a classical tripartite division into base, shaft and capital, and only *barely* recall a classical trabeation in the horizontal and vertical expression of the Chicago frame. The applied decoration, glistening in cream terracotta and dissolving the surface mark it as Gothic Classicism as do the thin vertical ribs. And so the building, which Modernist historians such as Sigfried Giedion have always preferred to the straight revivalist one, also turns out to have a classical ancestry even if a 'crooked' one. Perhaps a side benefit of the present classical period is that it allows us to once again enjoy such old favourites but for new reasons. Certainly Post-Modernism has forced a general revaluing of Pre-Modernists, the generation just prior to that of the 1920s, and so we can find new motives for appreciating the early Mies before he went Modern.

Mies' Perls House, Berlin, 1911, or his project for the Kröller

House, 1912, are both sparse, understated versions of a Schinkel-esque classicism that remind one of James Stirling's present work, equally severe in its reductions. We might term this the father of the present reticent classicism which wants to be very quiet about its parentage and cool about its intentions. Stirling's additions to the Rice School of Architecture, for instance, almost disappear into the background Neo-Romanesque (and are intended to do so) except for their occasionally odd syncopations, or strange lighting cones, or mannerist 'pilasters'. The positive intentions are obviously contextual, the campus is being completed, not fractured by a new building. But doubts may arise at this point. How deferential to the context must one be before the reticence becomes accommodating, or dull, or conformist, or all those pejoratives which Modernists hurled at their adversaries for 30 years. It is a real problem especially for a profession which is paid to create images of repetition and conformity. Against such considerations the recent Chicago classicism has to be seen, and we might start by looking at the canonic variety for this tradition is the most reticent and cool in its use of architectural language.

The undoubted master of this approach is, for me at any rate, Thomas Beeby. His Townhouse Project of 1978 was an early example of the new synthesis of Modernism and Classicism, describable in both terms. One might admire its circular voids whipping around the top like Bramantean wheels, or the layered series of positive and negative figures which march through the building as consistently as the Prussian structures of Mies. 'Mies doing Palladio instead of Schinkel' is one way to describe it, and how inevitable this conjunction of names seems to be. Mies was the Palladio, or aesthetic systematiser, of his age and so Beeby seems to be doing nothing more than following the logic of this proposition through to its end. Yet of course, aside from the archetypes (*the* circle, *the* fanlight, etc), there is an inventive use of space which syncopates in an A, B, A rhythm horizontally and A, B, B, A, C rhythm vertically. These syncopations are suggested on a front, which also indicates the real A, B, A cross rhythm. In the basement-grotto of the building is a very un-Miesian beast, a Hades face, which forces us to mention non-syntactic elements.

Beeby, one feels, is about to engage ornament and metaphor, but as yet has not fully done so. He has written brilliantly on the ornament of Modernists like Le Corbusier and Mies and as he told me in 1979, he awaits a programmatic imperative before he will design ornament. Thus his Tri-State Centre has only a structural ornament of round pilasters and square windows, a suppressed *Serliana* in the centre entrance, and topmost shells (which were never built). For all its emphasis on the round column, circle and square, that is classical archetypes, it could be just another Modern, extruded office building. Floor and window elements repeat without horizontal or vertical gradation. True, a proto-decoration is trying to

1   Charles Atwood and D H Burnham, Reliance Building, Chicago 1894–95. Chicago frame, *the* expression of Modernism, also relates to classical post and lintel framing; here also the tripartite organisation, symmetries, decoration and ribs are Free Style Classical.
2   James Stirling & Michael Wilford, Rice University. School of Architecture, Houston, Expansion, 1980–81. 'Neo-Romanesque' with asymmetries, cones of light, horizontal 'Modernist' windows combined with classicism in a free style manner (ph: Val Glitsch)
3   Thomas Beeby, Townhouse Project, Chicago, 1978. Adamesque and Palladian elements fused with a Miesian structural ordering
4, 5   Thomas Beeby, (Hammond, Beeby, Babka), Tri-State Center, Northbrook, Illinois, 1978–79. Square windows, circular columns and pilasters, *Serliana* (without its decorative shell) on a Modernist office of five equal floors. All elevations are symmetrical, but the syntax is treated in a Modernist, or endless way, as it runs on without beginning or end (ph: Howard N Kaplan)

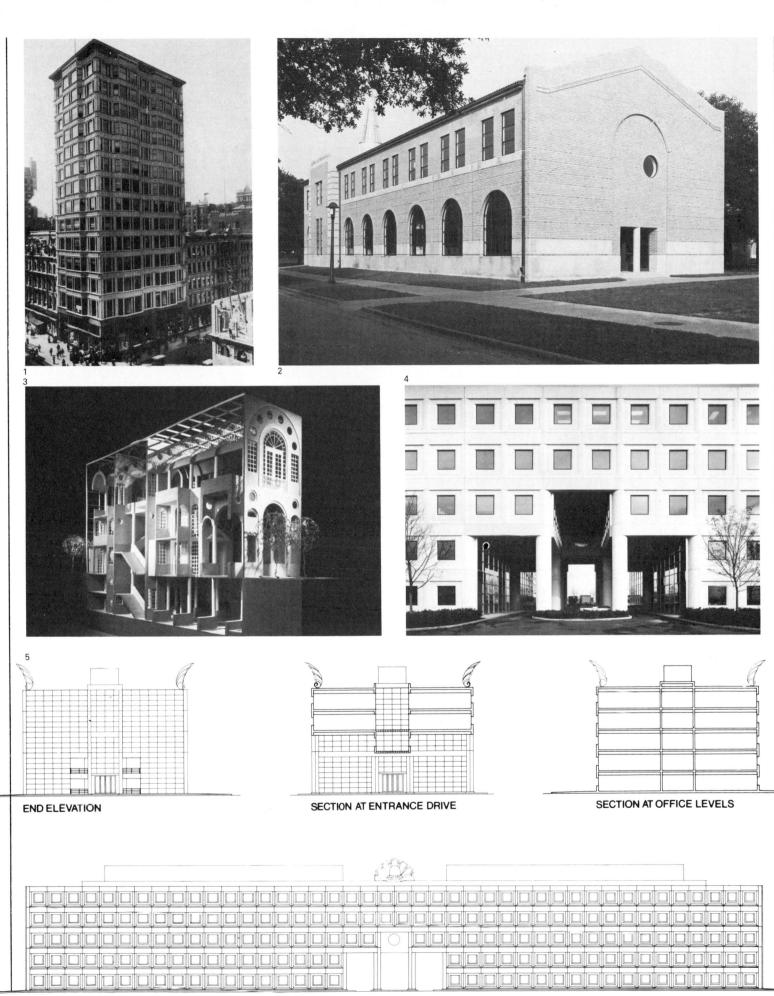

1

2

3

4

5

END ELEVATION

SECTION AT ENTRANCE DRIVE

SECTION AT OFFICE LEVELS

get out of the construction, as we feel the beginnings of column and entablature, but it is never allowed to do so. Positively this has a heroic, fundamentalist sobriety, negatively a timid reticence. Should we praise Beeby for his classical *gravitas*, or fault him for the boredom? We can, and probably will, do both in turn depending on our mood and how much regular architecture we have recently experienced. This contextualism of a different sort, of architectural judgement, points to the obvious fact that we judge a building by its relations to others and the statistical mix of the environment. When it becomes too filled with regular, symmetrical offices of a slightly grand type (as all the Chicago classicists seem intent on filling it) then we will welcome back those lightweight structures which the Chicago architects of the 1930s produced (Fuller, Goldberg and the Kecks).

American classicism has always had a brittle, precise, hard-edge quality when compared with its European counterpart. Vincent Scully has identified this 'precisionist' strain which we can see, for instance, in Henry Bacon's memorial for Abraham Lincoln, 1922. The same crisp style characterises these classicists who used to be Miesians. Laurence Booth stretches thin white and silver trim over a taut skin of stucco and glass, as if it were still the 1920s, but now the specific forms happen to be classical not International Style. The Lione House etches floor lines and keystones in a mechanical way, and the dark blank flatness of the window arches makes this Palladian window into a machine-tooled abstraction. Frank Stella and his hard-edge architect friend Richard Meier seem to be behind this cool manner. Booth's Adams Road Villa is another reticent cross between a thin mechanical imagery and set of classical archetypes – symmetrical plan, exedra, loggia, and Phileban forms. Here is the Mies of the Kröller House, here are the Pre-Modernists such as Loos who spurned decoration. (Booth chastises the 'tail-fin period' of Post-Modern Classicism.) It is true that voussoirs and keystone flare out over an entrance arch, but otherwise the classicism is subdued and universalised. One must recall in this context the idea of J J P Oud's 'unhistorical classicism' based on following 'the mechanical methods of production', plus the aesthetic of harmonious integration (Alberti). Booth, like Oud, might say 'all decoration is inessential, mere outward compensation for inner impotence' although from his generalising standpoint of the 1980s (and allowing for his etched decoration). His manifesto 'Gentle Synthesis' (1981) emphasises the general and collective in good De Stijl manner:

'Survival of mankind depends upon the regulation and control of individuals and groups to insure benevolent use of powerful technologies. Problems grow beyond the scope of only individual concerns.'
And:
'Overemphasis of small, particular aspects of architecture has created obscure styles, meaningful only to their designers.'
This last rebuke is a typical Chicagoan barb aimed at the esoterica of the East Coast, and it stems from an 'ideology' Booth wants to build up that will defend a 'noble and gentle civilisation' based on 'affection between men', where ideals of 'economic satisfaction', 'flexible organisation', 'energy conservation' and 'form and proportion' may be realised. This conflation of Greece and High-Tech with its definite male overtones, we may take as standing for much Chicago classicism. Its embodiment is most clear in the work and figure of Helmut Jahn.

Jahn is the young leader of the corporate firm C F Murphy Associates, one of the main ruling families of the older Miesian lineage (another being SOM) and in appearance he is a svelte Kurt Jurgens, without monocle, but certainly with the long German accent that emerges cryptically from between his beautifully curled lips. The strong physiognomic appearance is important because Jahn is the inheritor of the Miesian image – both in building and persona. (His cryptic remarks have yet to be reduced to the spare 'less is more'.) His work exaggerates a technical realism, as did Mies', until it becomes an end in itself. His segmental circle for the Department of Energy makes an architecture from road networks (the 'inner circle' of loops) from sun angles (sloping glass) and energy efficiency (the circle 'encloses a maximum amount of space with a minimum of material means'). But there is no doubt that

behind all this technical justification is a classical language. Not only is the circle referred to in Platonic terms that could come from an Alberti or Palladio, but the overall weighty, massive form stems from Boullée. Jahn's works seek the sublime. Like a vast, impersonal force, the river that shaped the Grand Canyon, or the *Zeitgeist* to which Le Corbusier and Mies appealed, it is meant to overwhelm one with sheer, masculine, divine presence. The individual is swallowed into the corporate womb and reconciled to the loss of personality, as always, by appeals to the collective, to necessity, to beauty. Impersonal Classicism and Late Modernism meet in their claims to universality.

In his addition to the Chicago Board of Trade Jahn has answered Philip Johnson's Rolls Royce for the AT & T with a Mercedes-Benz. Whether or not this German iconology was intended will have to await a future psychological probe (or Jahn's admission) for the form is quite obviously generated by the background context and large interior atrium of 15 floors located (and signified on the exterior) above the 12th floor. The Art Deco Classicism of the original building has provided the pretext for the A, B, A rhythm, *Serliana* and 'radiator' cap. But most of it is in glass imitating masonry, and the curtain wall grid has replaced the old travertine stereometry. This fat temple to trade has an understated wit which is a response to the metaphors of Post-Modernism. Jahn considers his work synthetic: he wants to pull in various influences, 'be interesting as well as good', to turn Mies' either/or statement into a both/and response. It's refreshing that Jahn and his large firm can be responsive to pressures which so many ideologues of Late Modernism have resisted.

These pressures have been articulated by Venturi, Stern, SITE, Rowe, the writings on Post-Modernism and the polemicising within Chicago of Tigerman, Cohen and Pran. These last three, who operate very differently, nevertheless can be considered as similar in some important respects: they draw their classicism freehand, they make cultural not technological arguments for their forms, and they allow, even seek out, influences from abroad (which means outside of Chicago) that make their classicism Free Style.

Stuart Cohen, the historian among architects, has studied with Colin Rowe, been clearly influenced by Robert Venturi, and has achieved the most idiosyncratic expression of classical themes. He says, as if to compensate for this non-Chicago attitude:
'My interest in classicism is an interest in "first principles". The elements of my architecture which might suggest classicism are: clear spatial and organisational hierarchy of both usable spaces and movement spaces, axial planning, and the non-structural use of columns as spatial markers (Alberti said they were the chief ornament of architecture).'
But this rather abstract and canonic set of attitudes is followed by a list of other elements which he adds to, or modifies with, this background: the residual spaces and undulating ceilings of Aalto and the interlocking spaces of Le Corbusier: *'The conflation of elements – some of them classical – that occur in my work reflect an*

6 Laurence Booth, of Booth/Hansen Associates, Lione House, Chicago, 1979. Booth writes: *'The Lione House recalls the urban housing of Europe and early America where color was employed on flush buildings of simple volumes. The arched French doors create a pleasant rhythm across the large front living room. A kitchen-dining room extends across the rear, complete with greenhouse. The simple volume makes the house economical to build and to heat and cool. Stone trim provides a pleasant contrast to the colored stucco'.* (ph: Sadin/Karant)
7 Laurence Booth, Adams Road Villa, Oak Brook, Illinois, 1979–81. Booth writes: *'Focusing on a grove of pine trees and responding to the movement of men on a footpath and machines in the drive, this house makes particular places combined with flowing spaces. Rectilinear structures form the ends with the major space being the "in between". The center is divided with vaulted "open rooms". The tower library counters the horizontal with references to traditional forms made with modern (stucco) technology. Window systems coupled with the tower, provide natural ventilation; advanced technology includes an active solar collector and a geo-thermal heat pump'*
8 Helmut Jahn and C F Murphy Associates, Argonne National Laboratories Support Facility, 1979. 'Chopped-off-Boullée' is often a rhetorical figure with a Jahn scheme. He takes a great primary form, the tapered cylinder, in his State of Illinois Center, then chops off part at an angle to give an unfinished look, an 'imperfect perfection'. In this scheme the circle is incomplete, and one side shows various over-lapping erosions. (ph: C F Murphy)
9 Helmut Jahn and C F Murphy, Board of Trade Additions, Chicago, 1979. A glass and steel temple imitating masonry and the building behind elides all surfaces with the repetitive vertical grid, a sign of the old Chicago's First, Second and Third Schools of Architecture. Ironic recapitulation as a Mercedes Benz?

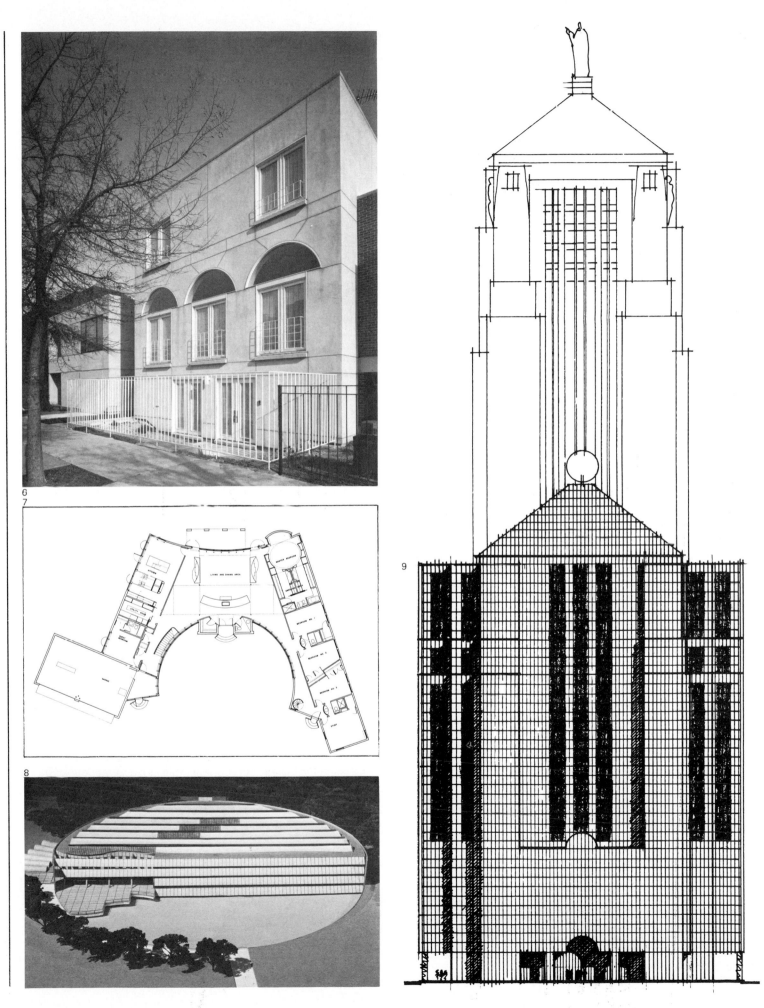

6
7
8
9

10

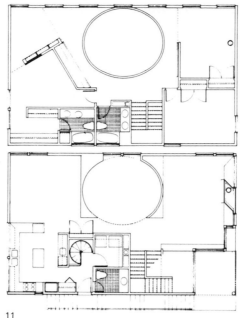

11

12

attitude which I think of as eclectic rather than classic'. The implied conflation here of classical and classic is, of course, just the point on which canonic designers insist and Cohen may be granting them too much when he also makes this equation. However that may be, his classicism *is* Free Style.

The Mackenbach House is a wood-sided box which elides various classical themes within a Modernist (even Corbusian) envelope. We can pick out the pediment and just discern a keystone above the garage, but the 'piano nobile', 'attic windows' and other formulae which Cohen mentions are undercoded or imperceptible. They are absorbed into the vertical wood siding, the boxed, Citrohan shape of Le Corbusier. Because the siding is treated as Jahn's curtain wall, as an homogenous form that elides things together, it smothers distinctions and semantic identity. This implicit coding, this coolness, is, once again, typical of Chicago and its love of the universal. It allows Cohen, however, to collage together very idiosyncratic shapes in such a way that we don't notice their oddity. The first floor windows and void above the door set up a powerful eroded figure, an L-shape, that fractures the box. Internally space nestles around a two-storey oval – undulates freely one way and gets a diagonal push the other. Here Rowe's method of collage has been appropriated so that classical figures, ideal archetypes, can gain maximum effect next to distorted residual space.

Peter Pran, in designing two hospitals, has mixed genres in an understated way so that they feel quite inevitable. The mixture of 1920s hospital style, the low, long, sterile horizontals of Aalto, with Gravesian Post-Modern – the red columns, slight curves and cutbacks – is however quite different from Beeby's combinations. Pran is beginning to manipulate surface, the depth of a building, in an almost painterly way and it's interesting that his lightly shaded elevations begin to recapture a modulation which several writers, such as Geoffrey Scott, find central to the Renaissance tradition. One can't describe these buildings in classical terms: no 'piano nobile', closure or bay rhythm can be found in the Facilities Center. The basic intention is not classical, but rather eclectic – as Pran describes it:

'Attempts to explore straight-line Modernism further today leads to the construction of buildings lacking in meaning. The limited number of formal variations possible within the stripped-down language of Modernism has been used ad nauseum, and since it is cut off from the past, it is very difficult to break new ground within its framework. Therefore, it is necessary to turn to the rich vocabulary of traditional architecture that people like and understand, be it vernacular or classical ... It seems natural to become an eclectic. Tradition conveys meaning and we draw on this ... Today a more informal, free style approach to classicism and tradition seems to be the most appropriate and successful.'

These remarks are rather reminiscent of James Stirling's stric-

tures on the impasse of the Modernist language and its need for enrichment. What we find in Pran's work is a true eclecticism coming from the origin of the word meaning 'to select'. He selects fragments, such as the red columns, and then absorbs them into a freely flowing volume, almost a picturesque layout (with, however, a flat skyline). His Bloomington Hospital takes a whole classical chunk, a portico with pitched roof, red columns, simplified entablature, and collages this on to a more subdued background of International Style Classicism. By reducing this portico to its essentials, a fresh but memorable image is produced. One is reminded of the *Serliana*, but it now has a pediment not curve; one can see Egyptian cornices and Schinkel here, but their presence is subdued into a new whole. Pran's eclecticism would thus seem to be highly synthetic in that it generalises and absorbs previous fragments, and doesn't allow them as quotations. It is nevertheless more sculptural, painterly and individual than the work of the canonic designers and reflects a cleaner break with the Late Modernism that Pran and the others practised previously.

Stanley Tigerman, of all these designers, has had the sharpest break with his Miesian past – a break of bonds which were so strong that he still writes letters to Mies and constructs elaborate Miesian spoofs. Partly this is done because the ghost of the master still exerts a powerful pressure on Chicago, one that Tigerman finds constricting, and partly the satires are done because Tigerman still is fascinated by Mies and wants to get him out of his system. If the proverbial emotion 'love/hate' is too strong an opposition to identify this feeling then perhaps 'respect/fear' will do. The ghost of Mies can simply not be exorcised in one generation.

Tigerman's 'House Done in the Intention of the Villa Madama' is, like its literary title, full of explicit references that would have annoyed the master. Not only does it use Raphael's circular *cortile* to welcome the visitor, but it orients this circle to the four parts of the landscape in a way that is comparable to the Villa Madama. One is brought through a sequence of spaces layered as exedra, hall and living room, roughly similar to the Roman villa (but the latter has grand, domed spaces placed asymmetrically to the garden facade). Where Raphael makes a complex set of spaces from figures, *poché* and landscape, Tigerman achieves a slick amalgam of these same three elements. Where Raphael's villa is an unfinished fragment, Tigerman's seeks the *partial* nature of several figures (especially the entrance colonnade and its truncated columns). Michael Graves, who has also been influenced by the Villa Madama, abstracts its lessons to a higher level of generality, whereas Tigerman, in a more raw, Chicago manner, likes his references up front.

We can see several of his previous concerns quite explicitly here: the favourite piano-shapes (now one actually embraces a piano) the undulating erosion at the front door, the 'dumb' detailing of mouldings, etc. Several of these references are meant to shock by

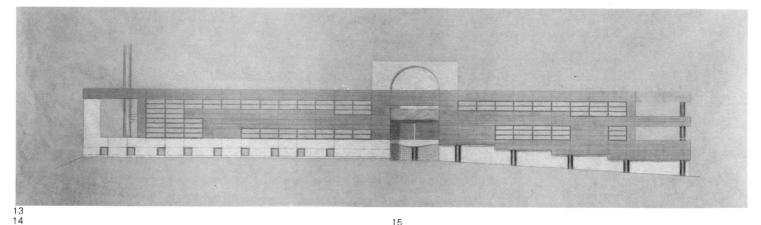

13
14

15

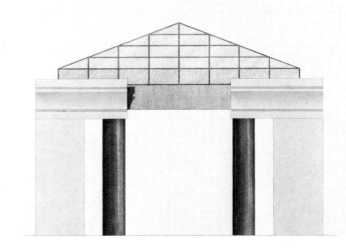

their explicitness, even flirtation with kitsch. Tigerman, like a Philip Roth hero, uses autobiographical embarrassment, black humour and raw emotions to entice and repel his audience. While this has led to raised eyebrows on the East Coast, where this sort of thing just isn't done except in a novel, it has also led Tigerman to an increasingly identifiable style and position – something of a rarity in Chicago since Frank Lloyd Wright. One can imagine Tigerman soon wearing the equivalent of a long, flowing cape.

Tigerman, along with Cohen, Pran and Carter Manny at the Graham Foundation, has done a lot to open Chicago to outside and even to inside influences – their exhibit 'Chicago Architects' in 1976 brought several previously overlooked designers to the forefront. One of these, Andrew Rebori, a very accomplished eclectic, seems to have influenced Tigerman with his heavy industrial swirls and representational ornament. Both Rebori's and Tigerman's attitude towards Classicism seems to be Free Style. Why not let undulations, Renaissance imagery, mouldings and sculpture exist within a High-Tech context, and occasionally be built with industrial elements? The proposition certainly subverts the unitary aim of the Second Chicago School which wished to subordinate all concerns to the structural frame.

In the sense that I have been using the term, Tigerman's classicism is ultimately the free-est of Free Style because it selects and combines from all systems without restraints (even those of good taste, it need hardly be added). This does not necessarily make it the best or most convincing: the more elements an architect absorbs into his language, the more creative and controlled he has to become. Borromini, one of the great eclectics, worked his hybrid compilations through very finely, not only on the geometrical level but also on the iconographical plane. It seems that Tigerman is opening the door to a Chicago eclecticism more than he is creating its ultimate masterpieces, but then this is no small or unimportant role to play and these are still the early days of a renewed eclecticism.

Chicago, in several respects, is still the tough, raw city it was 70 years ago, a place where Mayor Daley can boast that Modern

architecture started and then carefully overlook what it did to Louis Sullivan and others, a place where it is hard to grow old gracefully unless you are the head of a corporation, a place where conformity, power and fast money still rule, if not rule, architecture. Although the more brutal aspects of the frontier town and stockyards have been overlaid by an urbane sophistication, the general tolerance of individuality is not very great, the pluralism not very deep. Hence the reticent Chicago style which is quite identifiable; hence the flat, rigid, clean, fumigated classicism done with T-square and mechanical instruments; hence the Miesian classicism which has expunged every last trace of human fallibility, even presence.

All these universalising features are not altogether negative, to be sure, especially in the communal art of architecture. And yet we might contrast them with a more traditional, freehand classicism, that of Michelangelo or, today, Michael Graves. The latter has qualities which are more flexible and expressive, more immediate

10,11, 12   Stuart Cohen and Sisco/Lubotsky Associates, Mackenbach House, Bloomingdale, Illinois, 1979. Box with 'piano nobile', interior two storey 'rotunda', oval 'dome', 'attic windows', 'pediment', and barely visible garage 'keystone'. The open plan and interlocking section accept various set-pieces such as the oval, as incidents collaged on a background. (ph: Stuart Cohen)

13   Peter Pran (Schmidt, Garden and Erickson), Facilities Center, Indianapolis, Indiana, 1979–81. Long, low Prairie School horizontals unite a hospital building. A central symbolic arch, red columns and square windows are set against 'anti-classical' elements: no closure at the ends, no repeated vertical divisions or closure, no symmetry or discernible bay rhythm. Pran writes: 'The Facilities Center is a hybrid, meshing classical allusions with high-tech sensibilities. Distinctions are made between the machine half – identified by boiler stacks and the solid punched out walls (alluding to classical stone buildings), and the people half, with laundry, offices and cafeteria – identified by red columns and outdoor cafeteria deck'.

14   Peter Pran, Facilities Center. Pran writes: 'The arched limestone and glass entry represents a Free Style reinterpretation of images from Italian Renaissance architecture. The arch emphasizes the centrality of the entry and dignifies the act of entry. This major arched shape, which is proportioned to the scale of the whole building, also contains a secondary, undulating curve, scaled appropriately to human size. The building goes beyond the sterile Modernist notion of an institutional building by giving it a new image and a new poetic content'.

15   Peter Pran, Bloomington Hospital, Bloomington, Indiana, 1980–82. The entrance portico shows the thin, linear detail reminiscent of Schinkel's and Soane's incisions.

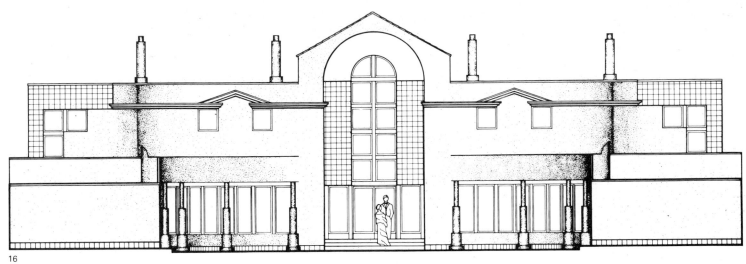

16

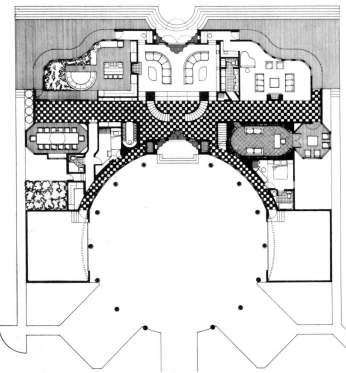

17

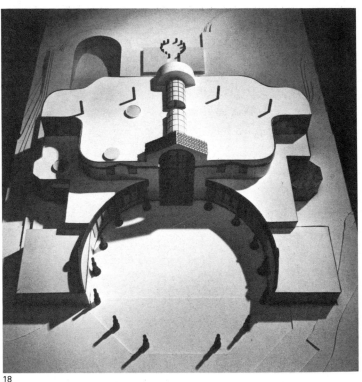

18

to architecture as an aesthetic and symbolic art which can express precise moods and meanings. This is a different kind of universalism than the Chicago Schools of Classicism seek, one that is based on the particulars of place and rhetoric. The Chicago architects are closer to the Greeks than they are to the Renaissance individualists; they keep their forms logically clear and distinct, general, slick, impersonal and archetypal. Given the right social conditions and commissions and a willingness to develop in certain directions which still remain primitive (symbolism, ornament and sculpture, to name three), these architects could produce works that compare with the best of their past – Richardson, Sullivan and Wright.

(I am grateful to Peter C Pran for his efforts in collecting the material for this article, which includes many unpublished papers from the architects. The quotes above are taken from these).

16, 17, 18 Stanley Tigerman, A House Done in the Intention of the Villa Madama, 1980. Entrance exedra pulls one symmetrically through the building, unlike the Villa Madama; a slick set of undulations and mouldings take the place of fragments and rustication. Tigerman writes: *'. . . the symmetry and anthropomorphism support a 19th-century humanism. The house and its adjacent "outdoor rooms" are thought of as containers into which the human being – not the object – is the central character in the linear movement through a site. The house is for a family of five with one live-in staff. The project is an attempt at the redevelopment of the 'estate concept', the utilization for one's reflection and the pleasure in experiencing one's grounds. In this case a croquet court, arboured rose garden, tennis court, maze, pool, gazebo and lawns are defined in topiary as edged spaces, the topiary edging of which is not dissimilar to the poché through which one moves to enter the library. Layering, historicism, poché and allusion constitute the thrusts of the concept'.*

ALDO ROSSI

The Blue of the Sky: Modena Cemetery, 1971 and 1977

This the most basic of the Fundamentalists' work is made from three primary elements, almost Neo-Classical and Phileban forms: a surrounding wall, a long house of the dead with pitched roof; a cube, 'abandoned' house with voided windows; and, on axis, a cone, the communal grave. Between the cube and cone is another wall building and then a triangular planned ossuary that diminishes towards the cone in reverse perspective. So triangle, cone, cube, rectangle and pitched roof – classical as well as Bauhaus forms – are reduced to essentials: the same tone, the same material, concrete. Shadow, as with Boullée, dramatises death. Indeed everything hits this note of finality with relentless predictability. Can death be so eternally boring?

For Rossi, 'The cube is an abandoned or unfinished house; the cone is the chimney of a deserted factory.' Perhaps many people will experience it this way, and certainly the cube 'house of the dead' is coded as a burnt-out ruin, without mullions, full of conventional desolation – a hulk. But a problem for this architecture, or any so reduced in cues, is the highly varied, indeed wildly erratic, readings it will elicit. When architecture depends on only archetypal forms it allows readings which may depend in turn on mood, experience and culture. Thus the oscillation in reading between those who defend it as a noble monument to eternal silence, and those who attack it as the image of the death camp. The cone can be read as both factory chimney and a conventional sign of the Final Solution. Rossi intended the first and was obviously not unaware of the second.

On the positive side one must note the measured order, the sequence of axial and off-axial movement, which culminates in the common grave, psychologically speaking, at the end of the route. One makes a pilgrimage towards this goal, past well-proportioned solids and black voids, through the labyrinthine ossuary which acts like the hypo-style hall in an Egyptian temple. And when one finally arrives at this chimney/Pantheon, in touch finally with the blue sky and death, the pilgrimage is complete. Indeed the whole sequence makes use of archetypes as familiar as the Egyptian temple and Gothic cathedral. The plan has, conceptually, a narthex, nave and high altar. One might only object that Rossi could have made his message stronger by contrast, by dramatising life as well as death, but he might argue that the surrounding context provides this opposition. CJ

Cemetery architecture. The cemetery, as a building, is the house of the dead. Originally, typology of house and tomb were indistinguishable. The typology of tombs and sepulchral buildings is confused with house typology: rectilinear corridors, central space, earth and stone. Only the most ancient forms in caves united the cult of the dead with that of the 'non-alive'. Death expressed a state of transition between two conditions whose edges were not defined. But the house-shaped urns of the Etruscans, and the 'fornaio' tomb, eternally express the relationship of the deserted house and the abandoned job. From that time references to the cemetery are found in cemetery, house and city architecture. This cemetery scheme does not vary from the idea of a cemetery which each of us possesses.

The scheme. The typological form of the cemetery is characterised by arcaded paths; along their route the remains are laid out. The covered paths are situated centrally and around the perimeter; they continue on to the upper floors and underground as well as on the ground floor. These buildings consist mainly of the columbaria; access to the lower floors is via arcades around the edges. On the

underground floor level the columbaria are laid out according to a reticular design, forming large courtyards containing the earth of the burial grounds. The remains are at the sides of the courtyards. As far as courtyard house typology is concerned, the relationships are reversed. At the centre of the area are the tombs, with regular succession inscribed in a triangle; this central spine or vertebra narrows towards the base, and the arms of the last transversal block start to close up. At the extremity of this spine are two elements of definite form: a cube and a cone. In and beneath the cone are the common graves and, in the cube, the shrine to those killed in the wars and the remains from the old cemetery. These two monumental elements are connected to the central spine via an osteological configuration. Only their dimensional relationship is monumental, signifying the problem of describing the meanings of death and memories. The elements define the central spine.

The shrine. The cubic construction with its regular windows has the structure of a house without floors or roof, the windows are without frames – just holes in the wall; it is the house of the dead; architecturally it is an incomplete house and therefore abandoned. This architectural work, unfinished and abandoned, is analogous with death. Of the four walls that form the cube, only one is 'closed'. The remainder have windows of one-metre square, with corresponding doors on the ground floor. On the closed side are tombstones, or just a large fresco. The shrine is a collective monument; inside, civil or religious funeral ceremonies are carried out. The shrine belongs to a collectivity as does the whole of the cemetery; it is an urban monument and represents the relationship of the institution with death. From the centre of the cube is the access to the underground level by a single ramp; natural light from the stairs illuminates the columbaria. These are placed on the four walls around a circular corridor.

The common graves. The cone dominates the common graves like a large chimney and is linked to the central spine of the tombs. They meet on two levels. On the higher level one can reach an elevated gallery, which is linked to the tomb path and acts as a type of conclusion. From the entrance floor a series of wide steps descends towards the tombstone that covers the common graves. Funeral and commemorative services are also held in this building. the common graves contain the remains of the abandoned – the dead who lost touch with the world, often people from hostels, hospitals, prisons, leading a desperate existence or forgotten altogether. To these oppressed people, the city builds the highest monument.

The tombs. The tombs are at the centre of the area. Composed of a series of regular parallelepipeds they are inscribed in a triangle on the planimetric projection on the ground. The elements themselves are progressively taller so as to form a triangle in section.

The plan develops in a contrary way to that of height, but along the same direction. The longest element is thus the shortest and the shortest element the tallest; the longest parallelepiped element which forms the base of the figure, continues past the triangle and, by bending around at a right angle, encloses it. In this way a shape analogous to the shape of a backbone, or some other osteological shape, is formed. Typologically the building consists of a series of corridors, on to which the tombs open; the same structure is repeated, where height permits, in the area above. The elevated walkway is open at the centre and reaches the front of the building; two stairs and two lifts which are paired and placed symmetrically allow the two levels to meet. All these walkways, which partly form the roof of the building, are paved in slabs of light stone. The part

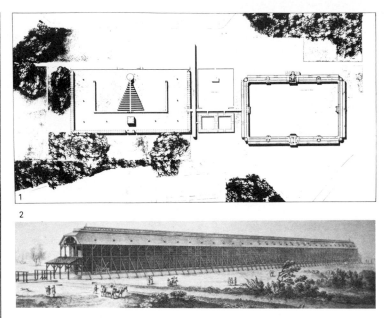

1 Plan of the cemetery addition. The Costa and Jewish cemeteries are to the right and the built addition, the entry arcade and coffin vaults, are to the West of this area, roughly in the middle of the plan. Rossi's design focuses on the twin monuments the cube and cone.
2 C N Ledoux, Bâtiment de graduation (evaporation of salt) Chaux Saltworks, 1770–1805. Ledoux was interested in giving simple utilitarian buildings a monumentality and he has appropriated the repeatability of the Greek stoa and rendered it in monumental wood trusses. Rossi and Leon Krier, in different ways, relate to this tradition.
3 Houses for the dead. 'Living death' is the oxymoronic sign of this architecture. The sign of living is used as an archetype then extruded twice in blue corrugated metal, voided concrete and concrete pier-screen (ph: Gabriele Basilico)
4 Analogous architecture, 1975, shows elements of the cemetery related to housing and city models by analogy. The 'architecture of shadows' which Ledoux and Boullée have predicated for the cemetery can be seen in the terrifying, 'burnt out' House of the Dead (upper left). The flat side, the steady, measured set of dark voids so well proportioned with respect to each other, the balance of volumes, the drama of movement have all been worked out.

which forms a roof is paved with the same stone, even though it is inaccessible. On the ground the arcades are on the same level as the green of the burial floor. The central path of the spine of the columbaria connects to the cone of the common graves, piercing it in two places, on the ground floor and in the elevated gallery.

Significance of the architecture. The conformation of the cemetery as an empty house is the area in the memory of the living. Certainly great architects of the past saw the tomb and cemetery as the exaltation of history, where the individual disappeared in the larger picture of a civil and public death. The Pantheon is a tomb. But in the modern world the relationships are much more private and the cult of the dead consists mainly of keeping memories alive.

Surrounded by memories or remorse, death becomes a sentiment and has no history. Only the civil aspects of this feeling can be expressed architecturally. From this comes the significance that singular monuments, such as the Etruscan tombs or the Roman 'tomb of the baker', have acquired.

Beyond this indescribable relationship the architecture must be presented with coherence as a rigorous technical fact and use appropriate elements: this is what forms the great Neoclassic cemeteries (Modena, Brescia, Musocco, Genova, etc) as expressions of a civil architecture. These references, in their entirety, are the meaning of cemetery architecture.

The graveyards. The graveyards are surrounded by wide paths accessible from the two entrances at the main sides of the cemetery. The graveyard has a stone plaque at the centre which carries the graveyard's number. The tombs are laid out regularly; a hedge surrounds the fields. The paths are tarmaced with a layer of white gravel or paved with light stone and lined with trimmed plants. The paths form two large squares around the monuments for vehicular movement. The paths are at the same level as the arcades around the perimeter.

Relationship with existing surroundings. There are no real reference points from the area or existing surroundings other than the existing Costa and Jewish cemeteries. Already surrounded by a

dilapidated district, they must be isolated by zones of greenery, large paved areas and a tree-lined path. The insertion into the large existing cemetery must occur by enlarging the perimeter without lacerations, while using the continuity of the existing walls. The Costa wall, organised according to the original design, will follow that of the new building. The general elevation gives the dimensions which the new complex will follow in its entirety.

Urbanistic insertions. As far as the urban connections with the city, especially viable aspects, are concerned, the ideas given in the 'General Regulatory Plan' are considered applicable. They show that for a similar problem, so closely linked to the question of property and complex urban decisions, formal external solutions are not a viable answer. The solution must instead be born from careful consideration based on technical proposals, administrative political choices and the specific knowledge of the situation. The scheme puts forward the necessity for a thick zone of greenery in front of the entrance facade of the cemetery building so as to create a compact garden, defined by a row of cypresses which follow a line parallel to that of the edge of the building wall. On the left of the cemetery, tangential to the road from Modena, is a vast car park in which there is space for other services or buildings.

Relationships with the city. The scheme's principal interrelationships with the city must consist mainly in its precise architectural definition, sufficient to constitute 'architectonic site' where the form and rationality of the building, examples of pity and the meaning of the cemetery, are an alternative to the disordered growth of the modern city. Like other public buildings, the example of the cemetery as an architectonic site is able to form part of the collective memory and will of the city. Thus the cemetery, articulated around the central graveyards, the tomb building and the perimeter columbaria, offers its dominant elements in the form of the shrine cube and the communal grave's conical tower. These two objects are references to the external urban landscape and mark out the cemetery.

Future stages of development. The rational and rigorous organisation of the whole cemetery permits it to be built with the possibility for alternative provisions in the future which would be just as valid. This is due principally to the concepts of symmetry and order, and to the planning of ordered but systematically additive layouts which in fact permit the addition of different elements at a later date. From a functional and aesthetic point of view, it would be possible to build the columbarium building first, and the central part later. It would be just as feasible to carry out the underground and central parts of the project, and later the surrounding buildings.

The cemetery as a public building. The group of buildings described is like a city; in the city the private relationship with death becomes once again a civic relationship with the institution. The cemetery is therefore still a public building, requiring the necessary clarity and rationality of its paths and a correct use of the land. Externally it is enclosed by a wall with windows. Its melancholic theme does not alienate it too much from other public buildings. Its order and layout also take into account the bureaucratic aspect of death. The scheme seeks to resolve the basic technical questions similar to those that appear in a house, school or hotel. But in contrast to the house, school or hotel where life itself will modify the scheme in time, together with its construction, here the whole affair is predictable; its time possesses a different measure. Faced with this relationship architecture need do nothing but use appropriate materials coherently, and refuse any suggestion that does not come directly from its construction; then the reference to the cemetery becomes part of cemetery, house and city architecture. Here the monuments are analogous to the relationships between life and the factory in the modern city. The cube is an abandoned or unfinished house, the cone the chimney of a deserted factory. The analogy with death can only be consciously appreciated in finished things or, in the end, in objects: any other relationship is indescribable other than as a deserted and abandoned job.

Apart from the municipal necessities, the bureaucratic requirements, the face of the orphan, the sadness of private relationships, tenderness and indifference, this cemetery scheme does not falter from the idea of the cemetery that each one of us possesses.
Aldo Rossi

RICARDO BOFILL
& Taller de Arquitectura
Palace of Abraxas, Theatre and Arch, Marne–la–Vallée, 1978–

A new idea in classicism is evident here. Previous constructional elements – column, entablature, capital – are now amplified in scale, divorced from their former roles and given new ones. The result is surreal, as one would expect, and frightening, due to the Piranesian scale. Some of the detail, such as the end pilasters, is outrageously thin appliqué. This scheme, and Bofill's Arcades du Lac, has thus received its share of censure and contempt – the annoyance which attends a new idea with radical implications. What is the scheme proposing?

Two almost revolutionary notions: that the most modern, large-scale constructional means can produce a classical vocabulary as easily as a High Tech image, and that this language can undergo an impressive amplification and still be coherent. The former proposition flies in the face of Le Corbusier, Nervi, Fuller and Norman Foster – that is, conventional wisdom on the subject. It is more suited to the permissive views of McLuhan on technology: that electronic media can vary production and produce any style we may desire as cheaply and efficiently as any other. This has the long-term implication, if true, that imagery will follow culture, not a technological imperative, and this is a disturbing idea for many architects who are used to justifying their role from the point of efficiency, or necessity.

The 'Palace of Abraxas' raises this issue so strongly that it will have to be faced; and no doubt the building will be attacked for this since it challenges a major ideology. In fact the variations in production here are minor and it is the overall conception which is significant. Concrete classicism can imitate stone classicism which imitated wooden construction – all stylised at different scales. No doubt the Greek sceptics were piqued when craftsmen went to Egypt in the eighth century BC, returned home and started building those Doric temples from continuous stone. A conceptual breakthrough occurred then also, and it was equally rough and ready.

The second innovation is related to this: classical archetypes may be wrenched from their normal role and reconstituted at an entirely new scale. At a certain point all creative languages undergo a deformation in order to stay alive, and classicism has certainly made all sorts of contortions including being stretched to Gothic slenderness ratios, but no one expected the violent disruption at this scale (12-storey columns). Not only is the ideology of the Pompidou Centre put in question, but also that of the Ecole: or at least the purity and decorum of the classical language as upheld by architects since Philibert de L'Orme. Perfection, nuance, suitability, ordonnance, refinement – all the virtues which might be summarised by the word 'tasto', formulated during the grand epochs, seem to be placed in doubt, or disregarded. The classicism is not upper-class as it always has been (according to its etymology), but proletarii, and vulgar to boot (as Leon Krier has said of this scheme). And yet there are qualities waiting to be perceived: a certain refinement in coloured concretes, the pure greys, whites and blues mixed with a strong modulation; a proportional system of each floor and the overall vertical harmony ($\frac{1}{4}, \frac{1}{2}, \frac{1}{4}$) seen as 'French harmonies' by the architects; and the ordered set of four very overstated 'French' figures (the U-shaped palace with its semicircular 'theatre' just like Versailles, and the triumphal arch and cour d'honneur).

No current architect except Bofill and his Taller would have the nerve and expertise to pull off these mutations in architecture. While many architects are redefining classicism today, and some like Michael Graves are even achieving a delicacy and sophistication with large-scale concrete classicism, none are doing it with

mass-production methods for an eminently Modernist building task: utopian, socialist housing. Fourier and Le Corbusier drew up plans for mass-housing as a giant palace, but everyone since has either given up the dream as a misguided and paternalistic nightmare, or failed to get anything like their dream built. After all everyone knows what the travesties of these dreams led to; that world anathema, the 'housing estate'. Only commercial developers and sclerotic bureaucracies would still seem to be committed to such leviathans, and yet in this lies the paradox for Bofill: it is precisely for such failure that his scheme is offered as a substitute. Will the 'Palace of Abraxas' take the sting out of housing blocks? To the extent that it is a French palace and not machine à habiter, or image of production à la Pompidolium, it probably will. However on an urbanistic level is one obvious lacuna: there is no escape from architecture, no vernacular tissue, no private, bungled, background building to skulk home to after a night at the 'theatre'. The most challenging question raised – Is this 19-storey palace suitable for mass-housing? – will have to wait for a survey starting in 1984.

Let us confine these premature observations (for the scheme is less than half built) to more modest points. The Palace, like Edwin Lutyens' Nashdom, breaks down the scale by using one building type on another. Here a basic four-storey palazzo (base, two storeys, attic) shrinks the 19 floors. By contrast the density of window pattern, the tight intercolumniations, the slender 'columns' (1:9 and 1:11 on the street side, more slender than most Corinthian) make the building seem even larger than it is. Giant 13-storey doors shrink it again, as do the four-storey broken pediments, while violent recesses and projections give it the superhuman scale of a precipitous mountain face. We will have to forgive the inhabitants if they think it is too big and small at the same time.

Contradiction (or 'inversion') is one intention of the Taller as can be seen by the accompanying text. We can find many of the distortions in the classical grammar which they mention: the larger 'urban window' which frames an urban landscape, as does the large 'urban door'. This last may open, diagonally, onto a new kind of urban square formed partly by the conjunction of central block and side wing. Columns now become 'inhabited cylinders', part of the bedrooms or, in blue oxide cement, an indication of stair tower and lift. It's significant that their distortions usually are based on finding a new rationale for the old form, because it is this which places them above formal conceit. Not, of course, that they are immune from it.

1   Site plan showing Palace below, arch in centre and curved 'theatre' of housing above.

2   The Palace constructed up to the 11th floor, June 1981, shows the corner 'urban door' and subtle use of grey, blue and white cements around it. (ph: Dennis Crompton)

3   Egid Quirin Asam and Cosmas Damian Asam, *St Johann-Nepomuk*, Munich, 1733–46. Free handling of classical elements, coloured stucco and, on the inside scagliola are refined distortions introduced into the classical language over many years. Bofill claims to be starting a new chapter with refinements in coloured concrete, and the incorporation of heavy curves from the Baroque. What if concrete can be made to evolve in such illusionist directions? (ph: C Jencks)

4   Edwin Lutyens, Nashdom, Taplow, Buckinghamshire, 1905–09. Two wings with a diminutive centre, slight bow windows, the implication of a palace front, and the tight squeezing of elements all dislocate the usual scale and make the building appear bigger (or smaller) than it is. (ph: C Jencks)

5   Detail of 'Theatre' showing column of glass, tight intercolumniation (1:1) capitals and curving out balconies modelled on Gaudi's at the Park Guell.

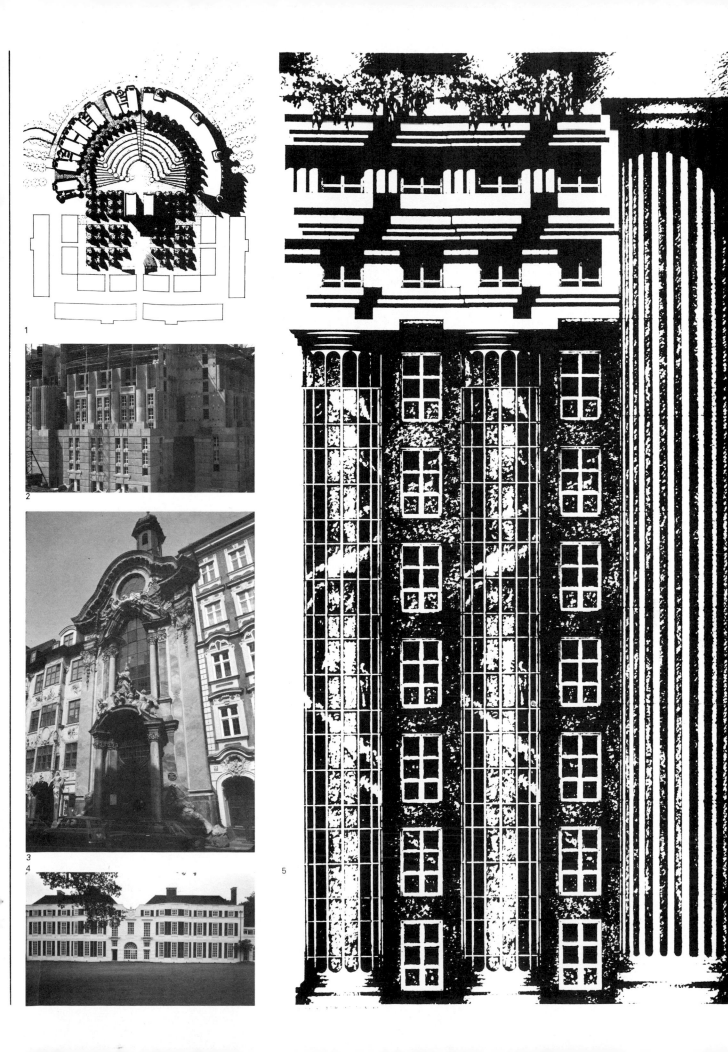

1

2

3

4

5

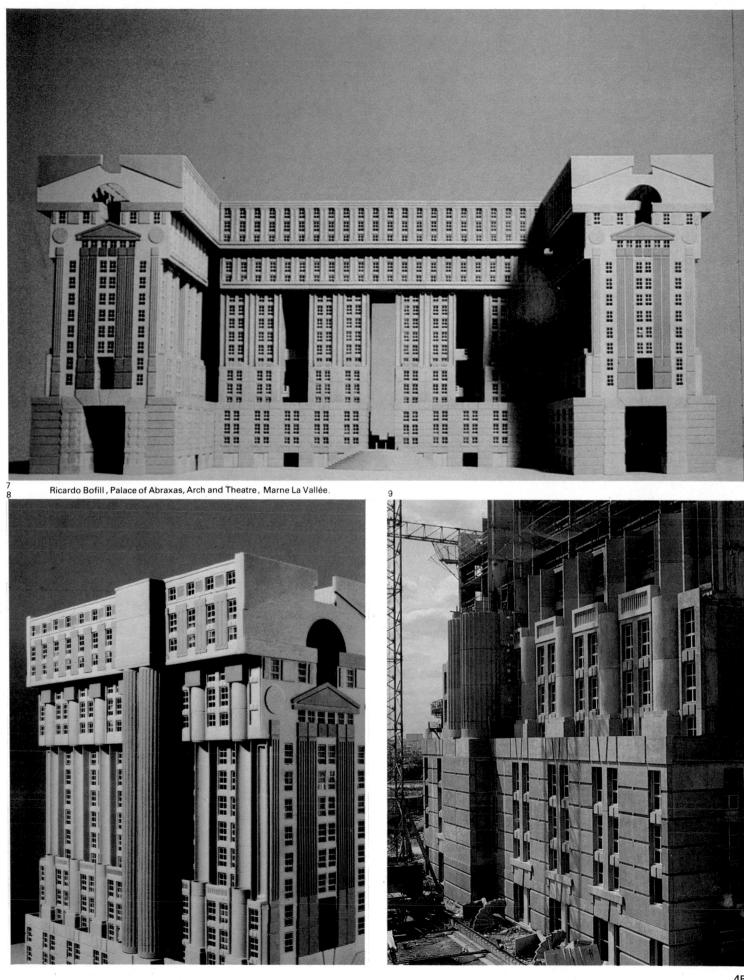

7
8   Ricardo Bofill, Palace of Abraxas, Arch and Theatre, Marne La Vallée.   9

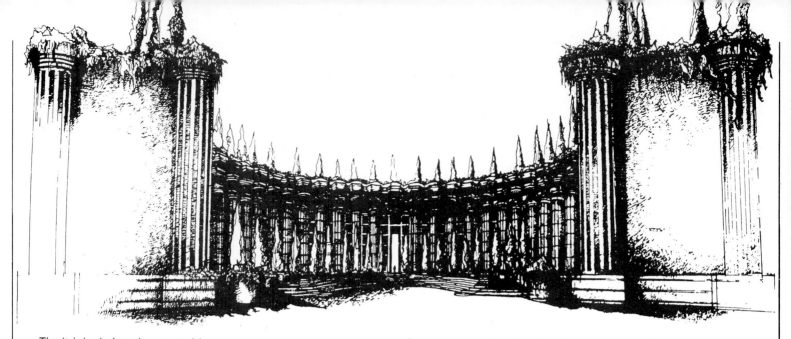

The 'triglyphs' on the street side seem, as the blue pilasters on the internal corners, somewhat gratuitous. But then so too were many acroteria on a Greek temple. What might have justified these traditional decorations, ritual and longstanding convention, will have to be formulated by the Taller on a new conceptual level of such forms are to have resonance.

What of the greatest conceit, the arbitrary monument as housing? Here decorum, bienséance, has been thrown out for the Surrealist injunction: 'the inappropriate is right'. Or so it seems. In defense it might be claimed by the Taller that these monuments are less outrageous than their previous proposition of mass housing as a cathedral (1971). But there is another line of thought which might mediate the apparent absurdity. Since at least the Place des Vosges (Place Royale, Paris, 1605) some housing has adopted monumental, palatial forms in France: the idea became institutional and so, the argument might go, why not, in the Age of Mitterand (as luck would have it) give the people what every other class has sometimes obtained? (One should note in passing that similar notions lay behind the working-class bastions built in Vienna during the late Twenties).

Perhaps, however, such argument is unnecessary because different images would be perceived. Bofill's set-pieces are coded in terms of other architecture and to that extent are part of the background of accepted meaning: after the shock of the monument has worn off people might see the buildings as referring to the background environment, Paris, columns, walls, windows in general. Forget 'El Palacio de Abraxis' and all that abracadabraca – 'we just live behind that ordinary sash window on the 14th floor to the left of the blue columns'.

Ricardo Bofill, the Taller and its backers are determined to avoid the dead ends that have destroyed so much mass housing and large-scale architecture in this century, and in doing so they will inevitably make mistakes and have recourse to less than perfect solutions; for this they will earn the contempt of academics and perfectionists as John Nash did more than a century ago. But the brashness of their solutions might be looked on with increasing tolerance, and let us hope admiration, as it comes to be realised that no other group is committed to such a grand vision and creative re-use of tradition at this scale: think of the equivalent leviathans, those of Seifert, Bunshaft and the architects of La Défense, Paris. Small, the conclusion might be, really is more beautiful. Perhaps, but then given the refusal of The Big to go away, in the last ten years, we will have to learn to design for it. The Taller is showing one way.

CJ

6   Construction detail shows precise finish of flutes and cement edges; the material has the hard edge quality of steel and the textural richness of stone. (ph: Dennis Crompton)

7   The Palace, streetside elevation showing syncopations and columns which turn from convex to concave. The extreme repetition give this a nervous beat. (ph: Yves Guillemaut)

8   'Palace', end view, showing paired blue columns which signify internal circulation (stairs behind one, lift behind both), and the overall reversible figure of the slab where base and top are similar. A certain Baroque quality may be detected in the way pediments are broken and they break into other forms. (ph: Yves Guillemaut)

9   Piranesian construction shot with stairs lying around like Roman ruins. (ph: Dennis Crompton)

10   J A Gabriel, *Place Louis XV* (de la Concorde), 1757–75. The revival of the *grand goût* of the preceding dentury shows the two main facades of the *Gardes Meubles* based on a variant of the Louvre facade. Bofill picks up the idea of the heavy base surmounted by a colonnade and topped by a heavy cornice; in particular he associated this with the schemes of Ledoux and Lequeu where there is, in addition a surmounting colonnade. (ph: C Jencks)

11   The Palace in similar perspective. (Dennis Crompton)

10

11

JOHN OUTRAM

Terrace of Factories, Kensal Road, London, 1978–80

Amplification of the classical language. If Bofill turns mass housing into a palace, then Outram turns factories into temples. In both cases a normalised language is amplified in scale to achieve an unlikely result. Most factories are anonymous, flat boxes with no pretensions, no presence on the street. Their bulk and economy would seem to resist all iconography except that of efficient packaging – Reyner Banham's 'flatscape with containers'. Outram has overcome this inherent image by extending classical elements: stretching pediments way beyond their normal span, making them 'avian' creatures as Outram says. These white birds/pediments hold no statuary or explicit images. They are dumb white corrugated sheet steel held in by thin black plastic trim. The proportions are flatter than the usual temple, just as the single-brick 'columns' are fatter. If this transforms the temple image into that of a bird or face 'looking on the street', then that may be positive. Usually the factory has no presence and it is precisely the intention here to create a public side for factories. Offices in red-trim wood are elevated above the ground level, which is given over to dark industrial materials and heavy shapes. The truck and car are masters of the ground, while architecture hovers above it. Seen from an oblique angle, the row of staggered temples becomes a primitive colonnade. By keeping the language fundamental it manages to have a suitable ambiguity and make more plausible the idea of workplace as temple.
CJ

Each of the five pediments along Kensal Road shelters a similar being: a cylinder of bricks. This ideal (Platonic) form stands in the traditional position of the statue in its aedicule, that is centralised on the axis of the fastigium. Yet the cylinder also mimics the role of the guardians of the aedicule, that is the columns, those transformations of person into pillar which became the Orders. The cylinder-as-column is topped by a black band, a mere incinerated residue, a stratified deposit of the reduction of its capital to its material equivalent.

The massive girth of this monostyle order, completed by its mirror image in the black glass, splits the pediments in two with a sexual energy, yet the two cantilevered wings of the roof remain, like an aircraft, inexplicably aloft. Notwithstanding this, it elides on the ground with the cella, and becomes a representation of the protected enclosure, the egg lying between the peristylar legs of this avian creature.

Thus Kensal Road plays with the traditional language of the facade to say that the gods of the city to which this facade is dedicated, the images that are shown within this aedicula, are personifications of the three mythologies of Modernism – the gods or Rationality, of Matter and of Vitality. This vision of Modernism has no room in it for common men, which is why the windows are black. Even with the energetic proscenium of their rhetorical red frames, they deny a role to existential humanity and reflect only the hurrying clouds.

Thus Kensal Road is a proper building of our time, in that it reveals our gods. The proper role of architecture is this representation, and the proper role of the city is to be the theatre of images in which the ideas and values of a culture come to life. It is ironic, but appropriate, that behind one of the facades of Kensal Road a company makes video programmes; for it is the proscenium of the tube now that is the aedicule in which (it is believed) our contemporary Pantheon appears. Yet who can believe in these disembodied flickerings once the transmission ceases and one re-enters the theatre of reality? Is not the medium of architecture infinitely more powerful?

The question which no-one will ask, and therefore which cannot be answered, is, why do we refuse to use it?

We are seeing now, in a few short years, the withering and dying of the city as theatre of images. With muscles wasted by inaction, the once mighty frame of architecture has collapsed and lies in ruins. In our century, the city, a medium that is as old as thought itself, has been energetically transformed, traduced, bombed and burnt out of existence.

Kensal Road is both a revolt against this madness and an epitaph for the values that justified it. One may be allowed to hope that it is but a step towards a more interesting end: the projection of the city as a living medium.
John Outram

1 Exterior view of units (ph: Jo Reid and John Peck)
2 Axonometric shows the five units having open space, vehicle space and office space beneath the roof.
3 Exterior detail
4 Idea sketch of the front. Symmetry and the monostylar front with end acroteria and a suggestion of triglyphs – the classical elements are explicit and tied to inherent metaphors of the earth and sky, as indicated in the layers of brick and the lightness of pediment.
5 Idea sketch of the elements: dark paving as water, brick drums, concrete frame, windows of office and broken pedimented roof. The archetypal temple with its necessary elements of roof, support and enclosure

1

2

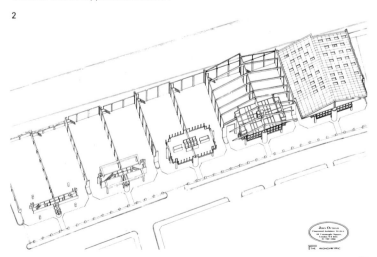

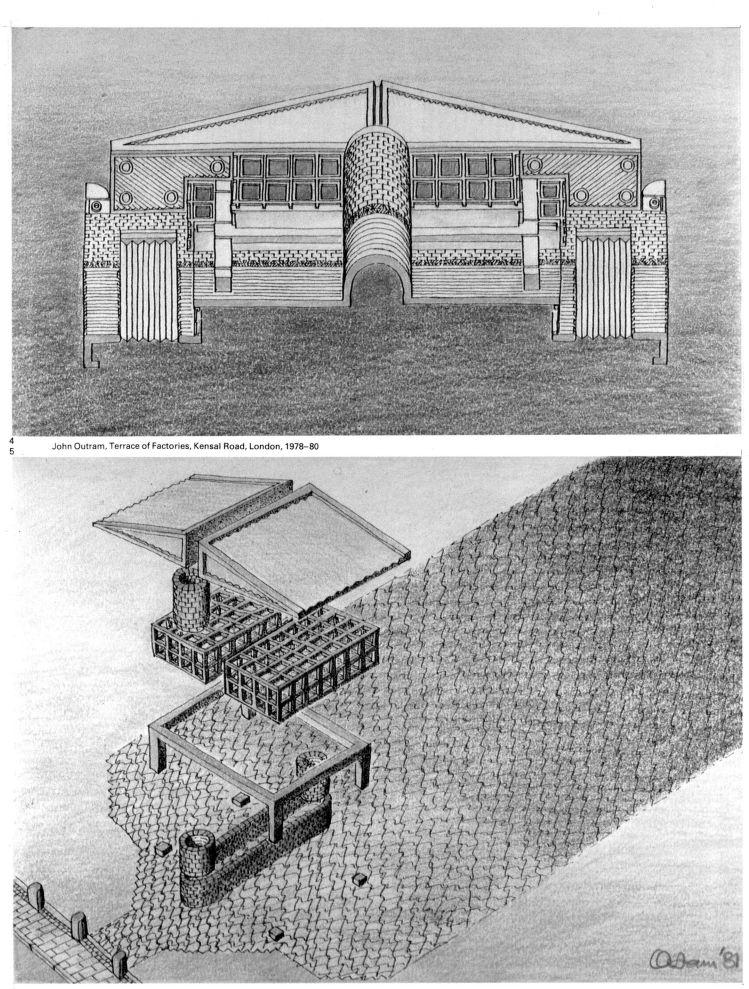

4
5   John Outram, Terrace of Factories, Kensal Road, London, 1978–80

BATEY & MACK

Kirlin House, 1980, and Holt House, 1979–81

Kirlin House (Villa III in the Napa Valley), 1980

Roman primitivism and thick wall architecture. Batey and Mack are the Fundamentalists of the West Coast, making an architecture from the model of old barns, the wall buildings of Barragon and the archetypal plans of classicism. The plans are Miesian by way of Pompeii. Symmetries rule, but asymmetries cut in. A vague, primitive atrium holds a basic impluvium: the peristylar order of concrete blocks may march off into the water (as in the Holt House). This sophistication of the tough hasn't been seen for a while and is very refreshing, especially in the California of monosodium glutamate. A basic datum is set up by the wall in both projects, a wall which has substance and may serve as a passive solar heater. Small square openings (hardly windows) are cut into the front wall: these give on to the more private wing around the atrium. The living room looks over a peristyle. Fundamental elements – tile, truss and concrete block – are taken up, even in the furniture. The parallels with Leon Krier and Aldo Rossi are obvious. CJ

The house sits in a low spot, dug into its site, surrounded by vineyards. The plan is an H-configuration forming two courtyards, one an entry space reached through a slot between the high-walled garage wings, the other a patio surrounded by public and private rooms orientated to views of the countryside. Built of concrete block, plastered over and painted a pale pumpkin, the outer shell is massive and seldom pierced. It also serves as a retaining wall. The inner courtyard walls are mostly glass. The interior space is open to the framing and broken up by lower room partitions of exposed block. The roof is of corrugated tin.

1   Kirlin Entry with parapet higher than a Pompeian house. The architects admire the enigmatic walls of Barragon, both sensuous and mysterious. (ph: A Batey)
2   Kirlin House, view to living room
3   Joseph Gandy, 'Five Cottagers Dwellings situated in a Valley' from *Designs for Country Buildings*, London, 1806. Primitivist functionalism based on wall, window, roof and chimney and given an absolute, symmetrical ordering

1

2

3

Holt House, Gulf of Mexico, Texas, 1979–81

The Holt House, with its 'Sixth Order' of concrete block à la Krier, again treats very simple ideas and materials in a sophisticated way. Unity of roofline and material is set off against the multiplicity of window size. A basic space module is varied in ways so that it can increase in one direction, and be cut into in another. The concrete block is like the Modernist I-beam, or ancient Doric – a Fundamentalist constructional unit. Here it is without capital or base but nevertheless with well thought-out proportions. CJ

The house is in a suburban environment and reflects the informal–formal contradiction in its siting and layout. It fronts a city road to which it presents an almost impenetrable face. The other facade opens to the expanse of the flat bay to which it gradually steps down with a series of unadorned columns to embrace the water. Half-way down the Gulf a pool reflects the sky, and lifts another level of water into view from the house. The plan is organised around interior courts, an atrium and an impluvium based on Roman prototypes. It is built of block and travertine stone to achieve mass and venerability, qualities rare in American new architecture. The walls are washed inside and faded Pompeiian colours, and the ceilings are faux-marbleized coffers. A very slightly sloped roof is clad in terne metal and most of the exterior colours are gradations of the same pewter shade.

1 Holt entry to sea; concrete block in tension (ph: A Batey)
2 Holt streetside: mute, ground hugging, enigmatic
3 Holt view of sea with cutaway Sixth Order of architecture

3

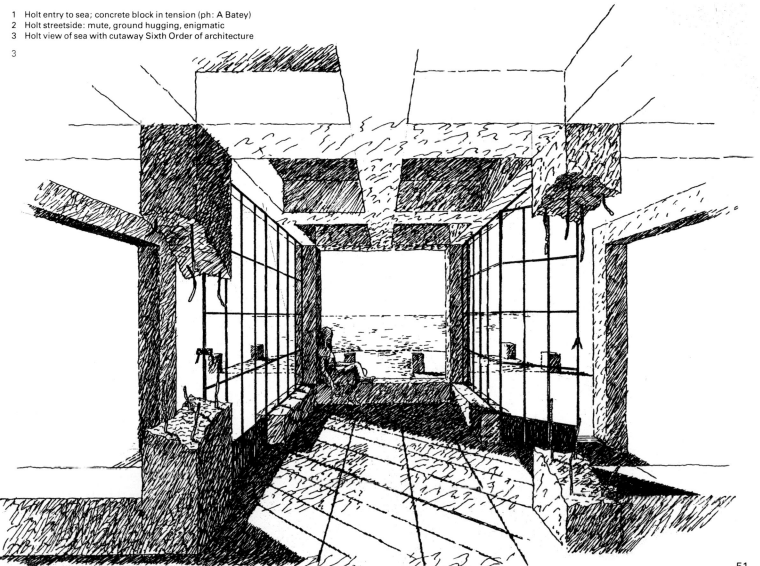

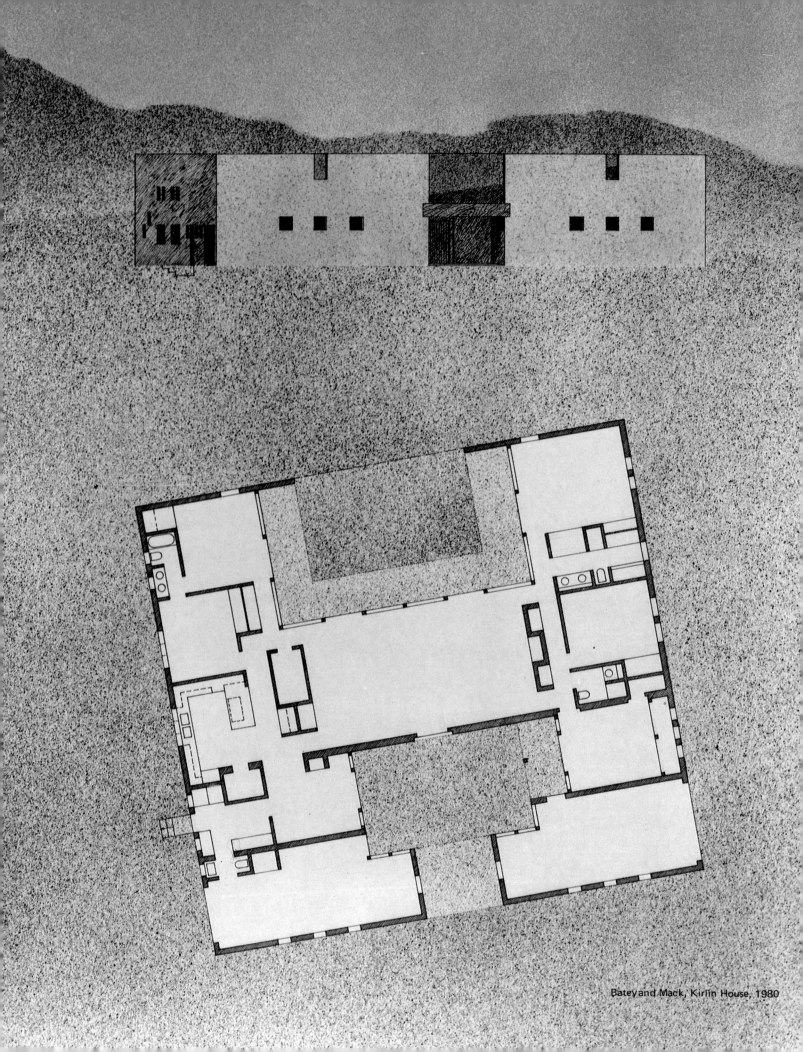

Batey and Mack, Kirlin House, 1980

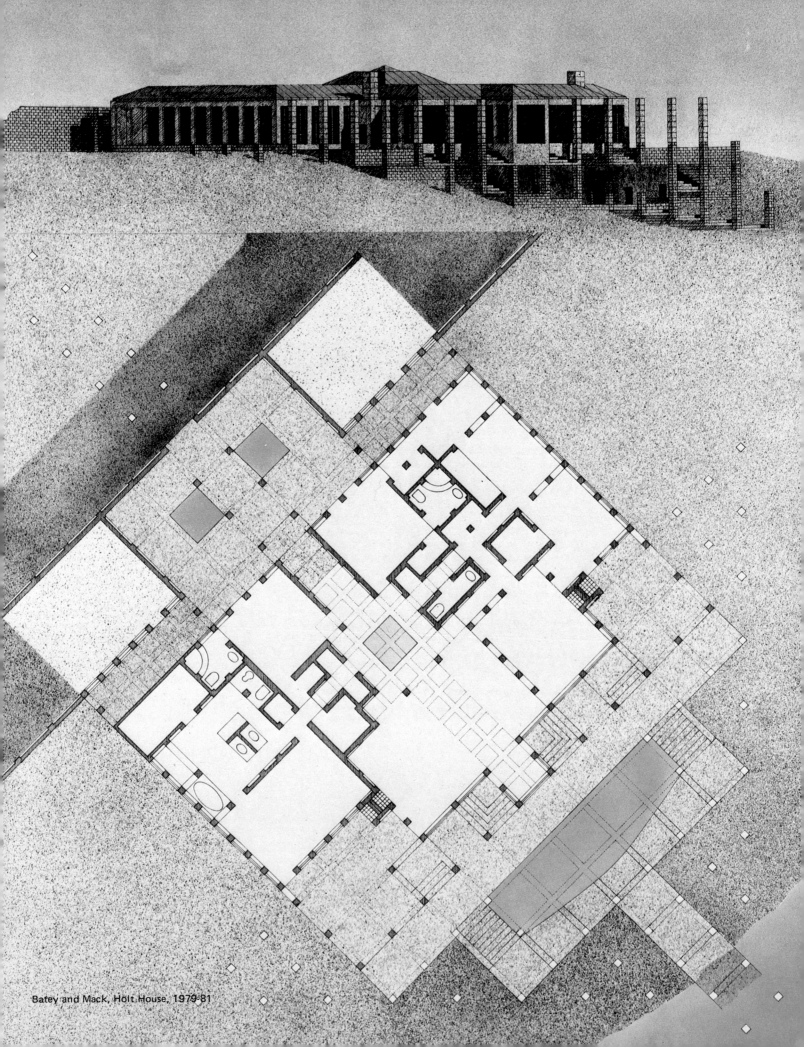

Batey and Mack, Holt House, 1979-81

MANGURIAN & HODGETTS

South Side Settlement, Columbus, Ohio, 1978–80

This community centre has, like Leon Krier's School for Five Hundred Children, a village-type plan. Large scale elements – the pitched roof meeting room and gym – are huddled together on a grid plan reminiscent of the monastery of St Gall. Several important volumes break off from the grid while axial and non-axial directions are stressed in turn. The organisation of set pieces on a route recalls the Hadrianic planning so prevalent at the moment.

The Fundamentalist concrete block is treated as the main icon while grey ('real') materials such as cement asbestos board and spiral ribbed tubes harmonise with it. This realism, combined with the honest expression of actual construction (note the pediment cut and stepped to reveal the truth) tie the work to Brutalism as well as the Ticino school of architects led by Rossi and Reinhardt and Reichlin. A good deal of anticipation is set up by the way glimpses of further buildings are partly revealed. The compacting of elements tightly together thus results in a tough, village drama suitable to the realities of a modest neighbourhood. CJ

This structure in Columbus, Ohio, is composed of concrete block walls and a variety of roofs. The principal spaces lie along an east-west axis, broken at the eastern end. There is a rectangular space with a peaked roof, called the Meeting Room; a nearly square space with no roof, called the Courtyard; a cubicle space with a vaulted roof, called the Central Building; and another nearly square space with a roof, called the Gymnasium. These spaces, bound by long parallel structures to the north and south, are in turn surrounded by the smaller wooden structures which are common in this part of the country.

There are four semicycles, each 22 feet across. Each is made of masonry units. Two are placed symmetrically on either side of the Central Building. Another acts as a freestanding proscenium at the eastern end of the Courtyard. The fourth is the vault itself. In each case, they have been turned so that their open side faces the major adjacent space.

The principal entrance is provided at the eastern end by a ramp, which rises to the central opening in the proscenium wall, and a path, which parallels the ramp at grade and gives access to a colonnade surrounding the Courtyard. A secondary entrance, to the south, is marked by a rudimentary porch on axis with the pair of semicycles. The entrance to the north is marked by an ancillary structure on four columns aligned with the broken axis. There is no formal entrance from the west.

The Central Building is a 32 by 32 by 24-foot building of exposed concrete block, laid in loosely alternating strips of natural variations. There are three upper-storey windows and three portals of similar size on each face, for a total of 24 regular openings. The six exterior openings are closed with intermediate aluminium casement sash. The six openings overlooking the Gymnasium are closed by a combination of wooden doors and an arrangement of heavy wooden grilles.

Within this volume, and free of the vault which springs overhead, a functional object has been constructed of wood, metal, and concrete block, which penetrates the boundary at the first and second levels. A staircase and balcony lead diagonally down from this structure, penetrating the boundary, which is again redefined by a metal column and beam, before emerging into the southern semicyclic space.

The semicircular proscenium is at the vertex of the broken axis, of sufficient height and width to obstruct the view of the meeting room, which lies along the secondary axis. Thus it restores the rectangular form of the Courtyard. There is to be a staircase here. It will be the work of Alice Aycock. It will descend from the proscenium to the Courtyard in a thin tier, overarching a frame and hemisphere on the ground to arrive at a narrow pit fenced in a rustic vernacular. Braced like a roller-coaster, its structure affirms an alternative to the gravity of the building itself, while confirming the manifest reality of each.

This building is a point of departure for our work. It is not about research, or problem solving, or even doing a good job, although all are aspects of our intentions. The leaders of the South Side Settlement stressed their commitment to an ethic of integrity and hard work, which encouraged us to define an architecture founded on like principles.

Each of the many uses of the Settlement has a unique character as well, not simply in terms of practical layout, but in temper and involvement, which demanded an individual voice. The contemporary response demanded a subordination of accommodation to an overall formal conceit which would, hopefully, be perceived as a unified whole. The internal geography of a building designed within that ethic was to be signalled, rather than built. But such a structure could not adequately support the desire of each programme within the Settlement for a central place, which had essentially urban, rather than architectural, implications.

Therefore the building is a fragment of a city – albeit a minor one – where the arrangements are based on external relationships, as around a courtyard, or along a street, rather than internal relationships. The spaces are organised as though the structure represents the domain of many proprietors over time.

Within that framework, diverse geometries, materials, and sensibilities tend to reinforce one another to produce a composite, narrative quality which is neither static nor photographic; it is cinematographic. One must pass from space to space in order to comprehend it. Like a medieval townscape, the building is composed of an interwoven fabric which resists dissection. Thus it is difficult to perceive objects as freestanding sculptural entities, yet it is effortless to perceive one's own position.

Very little is concealed. Symmetries underline the essential geometries of each space, sometimes to quiet the necessary arrangements of columns and beams, but more often to provide places and focus for individuals. It is their gestures which must animate the mass of the building around them. And the building must only lend substance and meaning in return.

Robert Mangurian and Craig Hodgetts

1 View of meeting room and entrance ramp from east
2 Peyre and de Wailly, Comédie-Française (Odéon), Paris, 1770; 1779–82. Austere exterior, bold structure, fundamentalist emphasis on Tuscan and rustication, which brings out the stereometry of building elements (ph: C Jencks)
3 Conceptual drawing of central area. *'The vocabulary of this architecture is primary, simple, basic. Wall, column, beam, floor. Each is considered an individual element capable of confirmation within the totality of structure. Gravity. Light. Space. The memories, processes, and allusions which helped make it that way provide an important subtext, but cannot in any way distort the experience of being there'*
4 Plan; reading from left to right the main spaces are gym, central area with kit and stair, courtyard, lobby and meeting room. Studios are to north and clinic to south
5 Meeting room; note the crow step pulled away to reveal the concrete block
6 Symmetrical central block with banded concrete blocks and severe windows
7 Central area with canted stair and structure painted a blue-green to distinguish it; blocks are exposed on the inside; various activities, a fireplace, eating area, occur here.
8 *'The courtyard is laid out in the form of a rectangle with generous colonnades along opposite sides. Here the columns are formed of spiral metal tubing, and spaced in pairs, owing to the frequency of pilasters in the spaces behind. As it is expected that many gatherings of a public character may be held here, each pair of columns is surmounted by a balcony in the form of a monumental doorway'.*

1
2
3
4

55

Hodgetts & Mangurian, South Side Settlement, Columbus, Ohio, 1978–80

7
8

TAKEFUMI AIDA

Toy Block House III, Tokyo, 1980–81

Aida has produced several building-block houses which stress an elementary compositional principle. Like Durand's method the grid is followed, like Frank Lloyd Wright's Froebel method each pure element is considered independent and additive, and like the Shinto method the column and triangular roof form become the dominant image. Aida has even, in his eclecticism, followed the 'process' compositional method of Peter Eisenman, as can be seen by the drawings far right. Yet of course different compositional techniques may still produce similar results; hence the comparison below with the Château at Tanlay, which was built over time into a series of blocks (if not toy blocks).

In all of this we find a classic Post-Modernism, that is a hybrid between modern and traditional symbols and methods. Recently Aida has composed a Toy Block House according to Mondrian patterns, and thus the cross is even stranger and more explicit. Yet the result looks inevitable: Aida has found the common ground between Mondrian abstraction and classicism, or the universalism of Le Corbusier, Van Doesburg and Neoclassicism. De Stijl's first manifesto said: 'The new (consciousness) is directed towards the universal', and classicism has usually claimed to be universal. Two universals together result, perhaps, in a Toy Block House.   CJ

Architecture, which is created on the basis of realism and technological understanding, can be experimented on by a counter-proposition – fiction. *'Form Follows Fiction'*. From this viewpoint the toy block is an interesting motif because it is an interplay between simply formed masses, and yet it has the possibility of rich variation. This house is one of several that are designed according to this principle.

The site is the dense residential district of central Tokyo, and the shape is nearly rectangular, facing on to two roads. On this site an L-shaped block is placed along the roads so that a private garden results in back, to the south.

The client is a famous vocalist, and he lives here with his wife and two children. His practice room has a piano, and in the future it will be used as a classroom to teach his disciples. The wall between the living areas is designed to muffle the sound, and yet they can be connected during a party. One of the important requests of the client was that I design the house in the 'peaceful phase' according to the 'Kaso'. Kaso is a form of fortune-telling done on the house to determine its planning – it originated in China and is quite traditional in Japan.

Two entrances, the main and utility ones, were best placed on the southeast and northwest; the cooking range was placed north in the kitchen, the practice room was placed southeast while windows and mechanical equipment were directed towards the peaceful side.

Since the house was part of the Toy Block series, it is characterised by smaller pieces: some of them are fragmented like the one on the corner which is a lighting box. The playful bonding of blocks and the three triangles on the top suggest the variety of spaces inside. The congregation of pieces is meant to look random, and the colour scheme of the elevation was studied on the basis of a random number chart. Ten schemes were prepared. Each had a different percentage of grey on white, increasing by increments from five to 50 per cent. After discussion with the client we selected the scheme with 25 per cent grey.

The interior has a public space on the first floor and private space on the second floor. From the entry hall space flows to the practice room, living room and dining area. The terrace on the north of the living room acts as a sort of draught chamber and light well; a colonnade continues from the entry hall. The second floor is accessible via two staircases, one from the entry hall and the other from the utility entrance. The two staircases meet on a small hall which leads into four areas: the utility space, the Japanese-style room used by guests, the main bedroom and the children's area. Each area except the utility space has auxiliary space which extends and enriches it. These spaces augment the light and increase the draught as well as heighten the sense of privacy. Triangular prisms are placed over one of them and the Japanese room and main bedroom.   *Takefumi Aida*

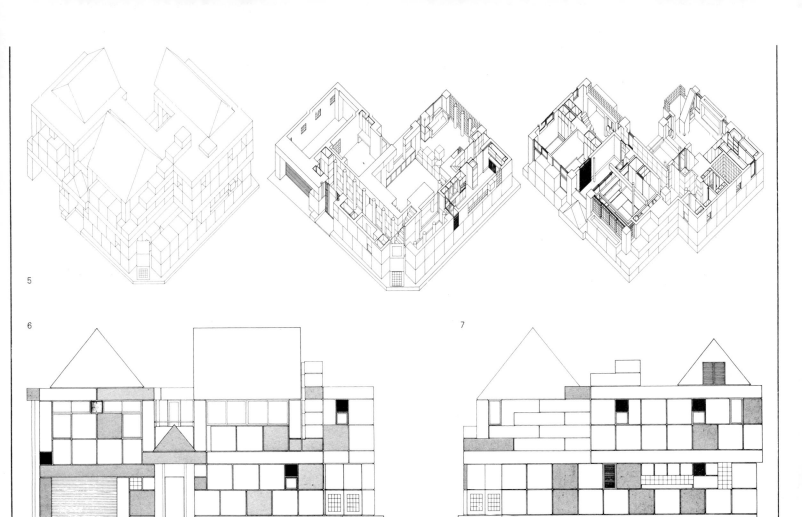

5

6

7

1 Toy Block House II, Yokohama, 1970, with central ridge pole support and 'Torii Gate' (ph: T Aida)
2 Toy Block House I, Hofu City, 1979. White purism in asymmetrical symmetry (ph: T Aida)
3 House like a Mondrian Pattern, Tokyo, 1981. The triangular prism slides out over the edge and provides an interior axial space. (ph: T Aida)
4 Chateau of Tanlay, Burgundy, France, 1550–1640. The French Renaissance chateau, built over a long period, locates several block forms around a general U-shape *corps de logis*. Rusticated obelisks, round pepper-pots, pagodic roof forms, moat, bridge-house and primary solids make up an amusing additive composition. (ph: C Jencks)
5 Built-up axonometrics

6 East elevation
7 North elevation
8 Ground plan
9 Upper level plan
10 South elevation
11 Exterior to interior
12 Dining to living room. Aida writes: *'The openings of the living and dining rooms are designed to look like crevices between toy blocks. The instability of elements is modified by columns, and the lighting system, using indirect and down lights, is carefully designed to stress the effect. The furniture is also designed along the toy block idea'.*
13 North-East view

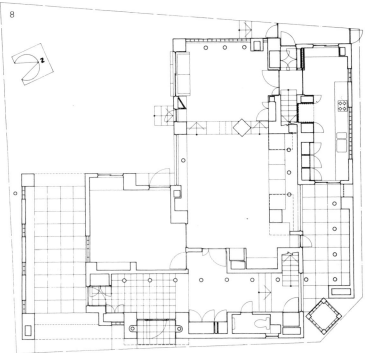

8

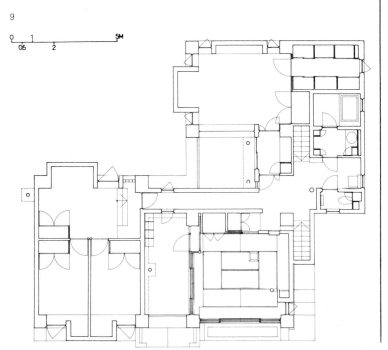

9

10
11   Takefumi Aida, Toy Block House III, Tokyo, 1980–81

12

ROBERT KRIER

The White House, Berlin-Kreuzberg, 1977–80

Gerald Blomeyer's article, which I asked him to write, disputes the label Free Style Classicism which I have applied to this scheme and tried to justify in the introduction. Krier's White House has a palazzo ordering, elements of a classical plan (both internally and in volume), symmetries, arch and 'herm'. I would argue that these five qualities show a classical intention to be placed equally against the Corbusian influence, which Krier mentions. And so it is canonic Post-Modern Classical, that is a hybrid, by intention. At the same time in its sparse articulations it is typical of the Fundamentalist trends. CJ

Some architectural historians have in the past few years focused on the relation between Neoclassicism and early Modernism. These two periods are admired for their purity and order.[1] Rob Krier's White House illustrates the marriage of the two but lets Modernism dominate: instead of being a Free Style ordering it is rather an hommage to Le Corbusier, an attempt to resolve Modernism's break with history.

Almost a decade ago Rob Krier started to proffer methods for repairing the urban fabric and working out strategies to stop its continual destruction in the name of Modernist ideals. Town planning had to become an art of 'town healing'. His policies were to mend the aesthetic, not the social relationships in an urban context. This work was especially relevant for Berlin where enormous amounts of historic substance were destroyed during the war and afterwards by 'modern progress'. Krier's suggestions seemed to offer a practical complement to the developing interest in urban morphology. His cooperation in several expositions finally led to a contract to design housing in the Kreuzberg area of the southern Friedrichstadt – once a location for Gestapo headquarters and other fascist organisations.

Since Krier's PR works rapidly, his designs were published and critics were just as quick to label the latest performance as 'Neoclassicist' in organisation and facade.[2] For historians like Dieter Hoffmann-Axthelm it all looked like transfer pictures: an ageless, timeless townscape without history and without an attempt to express things relevant for the district or local inhabitants.

What a surprise when the scaffolding was removed at the end of 1980. Instead of the expected classicism: the Modern Movement

had been resurrected! *'A journeyman's work with the repertoire of the 20th century,'* Krier calls it. The modern 'master builder' freely admits that many details are the *'digestion of my fascination for Le Corbusier: the curved stairwell, the two-floor loggia, the vaulted ceiling, the gently modulated interior walls and finally the white stereometric volumes with brightly painted recessed areas.'*[3]

The forms of the building in both model and drawing had been carefully identified, but the discussion was controversial. At the same time the intentions of Krier had been misunderstood. The different media and scale had allowed different visual relationships to dominate. For the tenants the whole affair seemed quite straightforward: *'The architect has a special name for this style,'* said one inhabitant, *'but I forget what that was.'* The general public in Germany has never completely understood Modernism. Consequently the Krier building is perceived as something strange, not homely. For the people living in the Ritterstrasse the building is best characterised by its colour: the 'White House'. Only one family said they had heard of it being referred to as a 'Mexican church' because of the mixture of stereometric and exotic forms, of white and colours and the symmetrical layout. The general feeling is that the houses next door look nicer because they are more conventional.

The layout is determined by the symmetry of the long central volume and a projecting pavilion at each end: a traditional layout. The axiality is underlined by a focal point above the middle of the central arch. In the front there is a blue cross with a tiny balcony having ship railings; in back there is a pink figure. Looking down Ritterstrasse the pavilions are a clear caesura so that the theme of 'volumes with volumes' (as an idea of contained extension) makes them into more active focal points. The whiteness and different formal repertoire underline the self-containment and the independence of the Krier house from its surroundings. Krier was the only one who gave up the brick base that had been planned as a unifying measure for all the houses in the Ritterstrasse. Naturally this sort of symmetry and axial plan dominate in the model and drawings, and leaves an impression of monumentality one thinks typical of Krier and Neoclassicism. Of course the facade designs also applied 'regulating lines' that, because of the underlying rules, 'give the effect of being more monumental' as Le Corbusier put it.[4]

In reality, however, things are quite different. The question of

1

monumentality doesn't come up. It is the low-rise, horizontal extension of the central part, emphasised by the continuity of the flat roof that gives the building its typical suburban scale – in fact it almost seems to diminish the genuine volume. This means it would fit perfectly into the modern, white Siedlungen of the 1920s at Berlin's perimeter. In fact Krier's White House is in many respects more closely related to the Siedlungen of the late 1920s than to Le Corbusier or the dogmas of the International Style. One need only think of Bruno Taut's 'Horse Shoe' block or of the fenestration in the housing by Martin Wagner at Berlin-Britz. Naturally parallels can also be drawn to Germany's 20th-century 'stripped Classicism' (eg, compare symmetry, axiality, bare columns, window grids to the work of H Tessenow) that later fell into disrepute as authoritarian and fascist (eg, in the hands of Tessenow's pupil, Speer). And with a bit of over-interpretation one can also find some early Dutch Modernism such as the several floor balcony columns (eg, J J P Oud's Tusschendijeken, Rotterdam, 1920). Krier's housing is, however, the first white building of its kind in Berlin's old central area and it stands in abrupt contrast to the urban scale of the district. Apparently this impression is to be modified by continuing this suburban scale on the northern side of the Ritterstrasse.

Rob Krier likes to describe the central part of the White House as a 'bridge'. To underline this image a flat false arch spans from side to side in the plane of the white facade. The constructive parts are recessed (except for the central wall/column) and painted dark red (at the side) and pale blue (in the middle) as if to dematerialise them. Factually, however, the building is far too small for the arch to become dramatic so that the bridge metaphor must remain too abstract to be understood. The arch is therefore as Krier puts it merely 'an aesthetic gesture, a unifying element'. The conceptual imagination seems a bit far-fetched in this point. Common sense lets the arch be seen as a gateway to the rear courtyard, a very common element in Berlin housing (eg, access to commercial premises at the back).

The flat white facade has an image of traditional massivity underlined by the rows of tiny square windows. This contrasts with the pavilion fronts where the visible skeleton structure seems almost emblematic for Modernist qualities (free plan, free facade, etc). But standing in front one can't experience anything theoretical like a 'duality of structural systems' or 'peripheral and central focuses'. In fact the building is too drawn out and suburban to enable such insights into Modernist (or Mannerist?) ideals. Instead the architectural tourist on the lookout for systematic aspects is surprised by Krier's disturbance of the geometrical system that links the main volume to the western pavilion with a 'cancerous' staircase window over several floors and with undulating steps on the ground floor. These almost playful elements surround the invisible front door of the building to the left of the central axis. The front door of the right half is hidden inside the other pavilion.

It is a well known fact that architects use different criteria to assess buildings than users. The impression one gets talking to the inhabitants of the White House is that they are generally very happy with their flats. Their overall quality is also appreciated by the *International Building Exhibition Berlin 1984–86* because they show alternatives to the run-of-the-mill. Opinions of both inhabitants and experts are controversial as pertains to the exterior. The tenants like the main staircases as their shape and volume differ from the norm and they function as a place of communication. The limited number and the different sizes of the flats is appreciated as a basis for an interesting social mixture. Some think the absence of a lift has helped to build up social cohesion.

The flats range from one to five bedrooms with three and five bedroom maisonettes. In his recent projects Krier favours housing three bedroom flats organised around a central living room. This spatial organisation was also realised in the White House. These types of flats have been built in Berlin since the late 1920s to minimise hall space. The three best known examples are Hans Scharoun's own flat at Siemensstadt (1930), Alvar Aalto's 'patio-apartment' for the Berlin Interbau (1957) and Oswald Mathias Ungers' buildings in Märkisches Viertel (1969). The drawback of this solution is that the bedrooms are only accessible through the living-room. The inhabitants of Krier's house are, however, rather sceptical about the future when their teenage children bringing friends home will always have to pass the social control of the parents.

This problem is well solved in the maisonettes with living-room downstairs and private rooms upstairs, and separate entrances for both. Krier writes that he based his design 'on the traditional Turkish layout', hoping that of the large Turkish population in Kreuzberg 'a large, black haired family would move in'. However, we met a typical German family that now lives in the eastern maisonette (113 m², three bedrooms) facing the Ritterstrasse and nevertheless feel that their flat is something similar to winning the grand prize in a lottery. The rooms are slightly higher than usual (278 instead of 250 cm) and the windows go right up to the ceiling. Consequently the light falls into the room from high up giving an impression only experienced in the popular older houses. This feeling is reinforced by the large living room (35 m²) that integrates alcove and dining area. Their favourite room, however, is the small solarium above the alcove because it is so bright and peaceful. It is the experience of layered space, the living with plants and flowers this side and that side of the window; it is a sort of 'inside-outside', a limbo between the flat and the outer world that makes this small room so pleasant and dynamic.

Naturally mistakes were made in the Ritterstrasse experiment and this complex has turned out to be just about Berlin's most expensive social housing project. It doesn't mark a turning point in

1 Ritterstrasse block model (ph: Wehrhann)

2 Ritterstrasse block as built; the central part relates to the rationalism of the Berlin Siedlungen (ph: Blomeyer)

3 Martin Wagner, Stavenhagener Strasse, Berlin-Britz, 1927 (ph: Blomeyer)

2

3

Rob Krier, Ritterstrasse, Berlin–Kreuzberg, 1977–80

Berlin Ritterstrasse Feb. 78 rk

Rob Krier, Ritterstrasse, Berlin–Kreuzberg, 1977–80

Berlin's architectural development or housing policies. Overrated by colleagues (positively and negatively) and architectural tourists, the White House might be relevant as a problem for architectural theory as it exemplifies the difference between the impressions that are communicated by drawings or models and the actual buildings themselves. It furthermore illustrates that Neoclassicism and Modernism can be crossed to produce hybrids that are difficult to put in stylistic categories.

The most important consequence of the Ritterstrasse experiment is that the architects have started to learn from their mistakes. The anti-Modernist approach of living on the street and the experimenting with new layouts for the flats is being continued on the northern side of the Ritterstrasse. This time the participating groups (chaired by Rob Krier) are trying to cooperate more closely to produce a neighbourhood with a visible identity while at the same time preserving the individuality of each house. One can only hope that the architects will be successful with their communicative training programme. This attempt to move away from the individually designed house towards a more process-orientated attitude in building might – in a next step – finally climax in learning to talk to the users. So this lesson aims more in the direction of an Easy-Going-Communication than a Free-Style Classicism.

Gerald Blomeyer

Notes

1 Cf Colin Rowe 'Neo-''Classicism'' and Modern Architecture' I, II in *The Mathematics of the Ideal Villa and Other Essays*, MIT, 1976.
2 Dieter Hoffmann-Axthelm 'Vom Umgang mit zerstörter Stadtgeschichte – festgemacht am Berliner Ausstellungsobjekt südliche Friedrichstadt' in *Arch+* 40–41/1978, p 14–22; also cf *Bauwelt* 43/1978.
3 All quotations of Rob Krier are translations from his text 'Architektur mit unverwechselbaren Charakter' in *Neue heimat Monatshefte* 10/1980. A similar English version was published in *Lotus International* 28/1981.
4 Le Corbusier *Towards a New Architecture*, London, 1976, 12th ed, p 76.

11
12

4-9 Ritterstrasse block, drawings and photographs

Krier points out his links to buildings of the Modern Movement and especially his admiration for Le Corbusier. The early Modernism here seems more related to the scale and the Rationalism of the (white) Berlin Siedlungen than the ideals of the International style. Martin Wagner's housing in Berlin-Britz (1927) also shows that an interplay of smaller (almost square) and slightly large windows and symmetry was certainly no dirty word. The dramatic rowing of elements/houses corresponds to Krier's fenestration in the central part of the White House.

The White House is a clear caesura of the Ritterstrasse. The pedestrian cannot experience the building as a whole as it is too drawn out and the central part is recessed and additionally hidden by the drawn-out pavilions. The colour is a prominent and nameable element, so that it is commonly referred to as the 'White House'. This difference underlines Krier's will not to integrate or 'play down' his building.

10 View from west (ph: Blomeyer)

11 Stairwell in east pavilion; white walls contrast with the dark red painted metalwork (ph: Blomeyer)

12 Ritterstrasse among the chaotic developments of the fifties and sixties. Terrace of ground floor flat on garage roof in foreground (ph: Blomeyer)

The White House

The position and the building in particular can be understood only in relation to my ideal project for southern Friedrichstadt. The building marks the centre of the northern edge of the block on the Ritterstrasse, and its facades stress the way the building is set back so as to form a sort of courtyard while the entrance-way stresses penetration into the centre of the block, where a residents' laneway is envisaged, leading to the Berlin museum. Where the dwellings project towards the courtyard it will be possible to add further buildings. The future laneway should start from here. At present a competition is being held regarding the building area south of the Ritterstrasse. I am curious to see whether my suggested division of the block, which is here already underway, can be extended.

I have proposed the division of the edge of the block into quite separate sites for the following reasons, the first of which is the most vital:

1) so that a number of jobless architects, including myself, may find work and put an end to the production of mass-produced dwellings, nearly always designed by just one architect;

2) so as to produce once more small residential units for 8–10 families who will be able to get to know one another;

3) so that every occupant will be able to identify his own home from the street or courtyard, or be able to make out his own front door, his staircase, his balcony, without any difficulty;

4) so that a multiplicity of differently shaped houses will once again – as in the past – constitute the image of the street, enlivening and enriching it. Only in this way can the function of the home be distinguished from the other functions carried out in the city.

It is very rare for a dwelling to be a bridge, unless it is completely subordinated to the constructional strength of the bridge or is found as a secondary element in the underlying base. Here we find both functions, in a miscellaneous fusion. All the stresses have been guided directly to the foundation, while the arch, both in front and at the rear, is merely an aesthetic gesture, a unifying element, and is the only feature reminiscent of a bridge. The central support is in the form of a slab which forms a half-pillar in the facade facing the road and ends up in the base-structure of the two kitchen balconies marking the centre of the building, forming a sort of inverted cross. The saw-tooth motif of the windows of the staircase on the west is made more interesting by a number of irregularities. The pillars between the windows widen out towards the top and the sills and oblique lintels are slightly curved, hence not parallel. The windows, which for the most part are recessed, are here flush with the facade.

In the facades on the side facing the road there are maisonette flats with a T-shaped layout and a glazed verandah on all sides. They are reminiscent of the traditional type of Turkish dwelling. Since 80% of the inhabitants of Kreuzberg are Turks I hope these flats will be assigned to them. The second type is based on the division of space into three sections, like a basilica with nave and side aisles. The measurements of both facades are proportioned according to the golden section (width to height). On the east side most of the windows retain these proportions while on the west side only the structure of the penthouse does so. The gigantic opening which marks a maisonnette on this side describes an equilateral triangle.

Many of the architectural features contained in this work were youthful efforts due to my admiration for Le Corbusier: the stairwell, the two-floor loggia, the vaulted ceiling, the gently modulated interior walls and the white body of the building, stereometric with the deep slashes of strong colour.

My rapport with architectural language is sensuous, so that I am affected by all the obstacles that this irrational source of creativity involves. It slows down the process of learning but makes it more intense.

Robert Krier

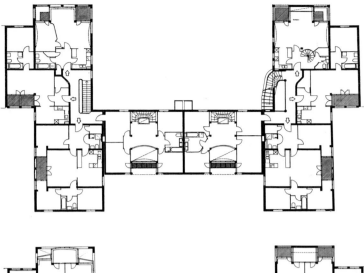

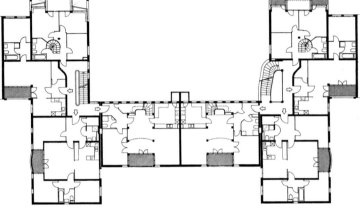

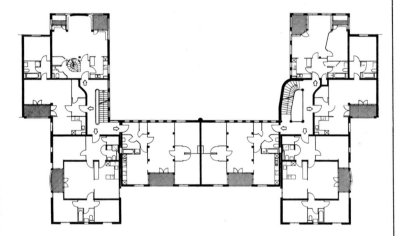

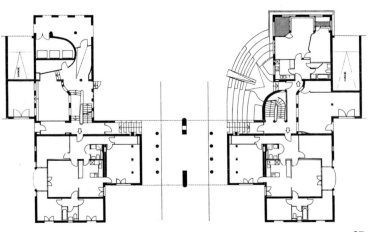

13-16 Ground and upper floor plans

VENTURI, RAUCH & SCOTT BROWN

Brant House, Tuckers Town, Bermuda, 1976–80

Venturi, Rauch & Scott Brown, Brant Summer House, Tuckers Town, Bermuda, 1976–80
1   View of bedrooms below porch and maid's rooms to right
2   View of large living room with *oeil de boeuf* and quoins. Note the flat Ionic 'columns' applied to structure

3   View of dining room to sea with lowered and amplified fanlight. The walls are painted light blue
4   Entry past picket fence to scalloped pediment. Stepped 'buttery' to left houses electrical transformer

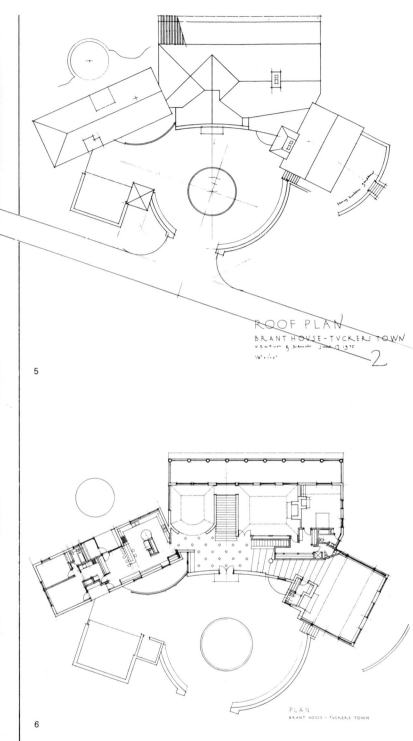

ROOF PLAN
BRANT HOUSE - TUCKERS TOWN
Venturi & Rauch June 17 1975
1/8" = 1'0"
2

5

PLAN
BRANT HOUSE - TUCKERS TOWN

6

7

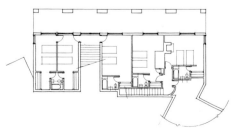

PLAN
BRANT HOUSE - TUCKERS TOWN
4

The cultural context generates the form. This eclectic classicism has absorbed elements from the white Bermuda architecture as well as the High Game of Architecture. An oversized scalloped pediment announces a grand entry to a modest hall and dining room. Oeil de boeuf and quoins accent the semi-detached living room, while oversized fanlight frames accent the view of the sea. Thus classical elements are used as accents on a vernacular background. This last consists of four pitched-roof cottages placed around an arrival point. The image of a village is thus achieved, to be set off against the image of a villa. This contradiction works to break down the scale and pretension of a house which would have been overwhelming on this site had it been treated as an integrated, Palladian country house. Amplification is used, as in many Venturi buildings, to displace clichés from their habitual role: thus fanlight or pyramidal buttery regain some of the integrity they had in the vernacular of Bermuda. Sometimes the results may look as 'ugly' as the Queen Anne work of E H Godwin, which is equally eclectic and personal in its distortions of convention. Here as well, a functional justification deepens the usage: for instance the porch form is used in a traditional way to shield the dining room and bedrooms below. White stucco reflects the sun while white pitched roofs catch the rain; louvered shutters catch the breeze. All these old usages are perfectly adequate for the old problems of Bermuda. The final result has that contradiction 'ugly but pretty' which Venturi seeks. CJ

Architecture today should glory in its differences rather than be made consistent to a specific designer such as Mies. We're more like Lutyens in adapting different styles to different sites and taste cultures. The Brant House in Bermuda has a very beautiful site overlooking Castle Harbour Bay and its blue sea. This we've tried to pick up in the light blue interior – which is so pale you might think it is the reflection of water. The building is *rather* correct in its details, but they are put together in unconventional ways. The flat 'Ionic' columns on the sea side are clearly appliqué, indicating their non-structural and symbolic role: they are meant to recall previous ones. The game to me was to take the classic elements, use them generally correctly, and sometimes, incorrectly – knowledgeably.

Robert Venturi

5   Roof plan shows village layout
6   Plan shows maid's rooms to left, dining room centre left, study centre right, and living room far right. Garage and transformer, lower left
7   Plan of lower bedroom floor
8   Elevation of entry courtyard
9   Elevation on seaside shows syncopated arches and colonnade and cut-off rhythms
10   Elevation of living room showing symmetry and juxtaposition
11   E W Godwin, Tower House, 46 Tite Street, London, 1884. The Queen Anne distorted classical forms by amplification and reduction as well as juxtaposition – as can be seen in these 'pretty/ugly' buildings of Tite Street. London vernacular is thus revivified. (ph: C Jencks)
12   House in Delaware, 1978–81, shows again a mixture of classical and regional forms. The applied, flat columns and giant fanlight take up 'almost' Palladian themes which are evident in the nearby classical barns: they announce the big music room on the interior and give scale to the house across the wide fields. Other areas of the house swing low to give it proportions more normal to the Delaware vernacular.

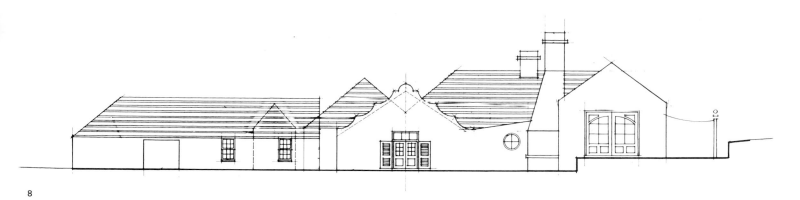

8

9

11

10
12

ROBERT STERN

Silvera Residence, Deal, New Jersey, 1979–80, and Hitzig Apartment, 1979–80

1
2   Robert A M Stern, Silvera Residence, Deal, New Jersey, 1979–80

3

Silvera Residence

The Shingle Style vernacular and classicism are merged together in a combination which is favoured by Stern. The classical pediment is even a vernacular trellis and it actually elides to the left with the 'dumb' Modern Box. Off-the-peg windows and picture windows are also absorbed into this inclusive aesthetic. On the interior a cooler, Lutyens-like set of classical distortions are mixed with a motif from Mackintosh. Again a linear shape is used to unite or elide different areas, as a white horizontal curves in and out of the fireplace and then shoots over to the stairway. The giant chimney-piece/small doors are a typical Lutyens' juxtaposition, as are the two curves set in counterpoint above it.   CJ

Pluralism is the characteristic state of the modern (ie, post-Renaissance) world, and in architecture the diversity and continuity of our traditions is represented in three expressive modes or paradigms which at once represent ideal and real conditions: the classical, the vernacular, and the mechanical. In order to represent the complex interaction of issues in modern life, post-Renaissance architecture has traditionally sought a synthesis of these modes.

Classicism in particular has two uses: syntactically, as an aid to composition, and rhetorically, as an aid to expression. Modernist architecture has rejected the representative use of classicism, concentrating instead on mechano-morphology. A genuine rivitalisation of the classical tradition, however, one which sees it in the light of contemporary production techniques as well as inherited meanings, is capable of fostering an interaction between a clearly public architecture and the viewer's personal reservoir of images and associations, thereby encouraging a meaningful dialogue between the present and the past.   *Robert Stern*

Hitzig Apartment

Fragmented, eroded and applied classical shapes are stretched to a taut thinness of one-inch wooden members. The airy white and blue forms give a Rococo feeling, although they are meant to harmonise with an Edwardian apartment. Indeed the slight curve applied to a basically right-angled architecture is a hallmark of Rococo, which often combined decorative fantasy with the most no-nonsense planning. Particular eroded shapes include the keystone within the pediment, the oeil de boeuf and 'Doric' column. Window shapes applied to blank walls (another motif influenced by Michael Graves, who also used it to lessen the claustrophobia of an enclosed space) and pilasters eat into the moulding. Cool cream and off-white shapes relate to the cheery Breuer furniture.   CJ

Our work in this flat, located in New York's second oldest apartment house, involved the reconfiguration of one-half of the available space (that devoted to sleeping, bathing and cooking) in order to attempt to bring that space up to a level of artistic excellence commensurate with the rest which consists of two magnificently proportioned, irregularly configured and interestingly detailed Edwardian rooms.   *Robert Stern*

(All photos Edmund H Stoecklin)

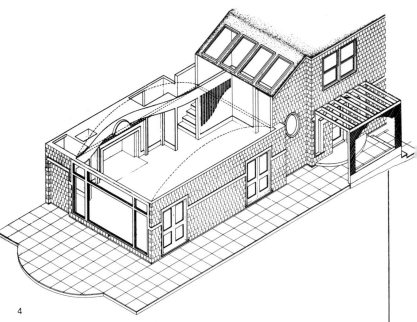

4

1   Silvera fireplace and living room. Curve and counter-curve in cream are interlaced with thin, white classical elements in a very elegant and intriguing way.
2   Exterior patio of the Silvera house shows a broken pediment of trellis that merges with Modernist rectangles to the left. (ph: Robert Lautman)
3   Silvera House has a Mackintosh stairway that is effectively top-lit. Stern is quite prepared to lift design motifs straight when he thinks he can't improve them.
4   Axonometric shows the collage of vernacular planning and classical appliqué. Note the unifying, continous linear curve on the interior.
5   Hitzig Apartment elevations and plan
6   Hitzig apartment window wall hides the kitchen, but space is allowed to flow into it from the side and top. Post-Modern spatial layering is combined with erosions here to give the illusion of greater depth. (ph: Edmund Stoecklin)
7, 8   Hard-edge moulding syncopates with the geometry of the functional volumes in a way that recalls Frank Lloyd Wright; decoration is kept flat, simple, volumetric and cheap (ph: Edmund Stoecklin)
9   Edwardian apartment to left, Post-Modern Classical straight ahead (which hides kitchen) and Modern Breuer in the foreground
10   Erosion of Doric column allows glimpse of space which also flows over mouldings at the top.

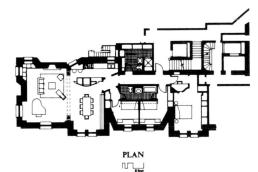

PLAN

5

INTERIOR ELEVATIONS

HITZIG APARTMENT RENOVATION

6
7
    Robert A M Stern, Hitzig apartment, New York, 1979–80

8

9
10

HANNS KAINZ

Jessica McClintock Retail Store
San Francisco, 1980–81

1

Project team included Hanns Kainz T C Chen, Ciina M Feng and Jennifer Ferguson.

Commercial illusionism. As with the work of Hans Hollein, whom Kainz knows from his Austrian days, there is one disturbing aspect: society does not offer such witty design talent more exacting building tasks than candle shops and boutiques. Kainz shows himself to be equal to the Viennese designers of such small-scale jewels – the intricate work of Wagner, Loos and Hofmann – and like them he is able to design with conceptual clarity and brilliant detail.

Here the shop front sets up the eroded figure of a Serliana, *which is then extruded through the nave of the building in a series of screens. This figure, a familiar sign of window and door, is used conventionally to signify these things, but it is also combined with other traditional elements: keystone and alternating bands of (glasscrete) rustication. Like Hawksmoor's rustication, it is an inventive combination of usually disparate pieces, enjoyed for its pure architectonic power. To accentuate the illusionism of this wall, Kainz has pulled it away from the glass wall behind, and shown its actual glasscrete section and reinforcing. Thus he makes a drama not only from the* trompe l'oeil, *but also from the reality behind it – a double artfulness. Throughout illusion and reality, classicism and commercialism, real salesgirls and mannikins offer us the same duality, which is probably fitting for the function. 'Concrete' trusses visually keep the walls from falling in during an earthquake and then sit daintily above a hard-edge dentil frieze revealing their true insubstantiality. Linoleum and marble, Brutalist concrete and strip lighting, 'mirror arcade' and warped perspective, rough and smooth*

– all the amusing and sensuous oppositions one could want in such a small space. Kainz speaks of the building in almost religious terms ('transept and nave'), and after having experienced the beauty and delight of this space one can only hope that a church will be his next commission.   CJ

Programme and objectives. Jessica McClintock, a fashion designer, well known and very successful on the scale of manufacturing ladies' apparel in San Francisco, decided that the time was ripe to challenge the growing fashion retail scene in downtown San Francisco by opening a specialty boutique featuring her own designer labels. Chosen as a site was a very small and exquisite pipe and tobacco shop, well remembered by style-conscious San Franciscans from earlier days. The shop had closed its doors after having barely managed to survive the 1970s, a period during which another newcomer in fashion retail, located opposite the street on the same block of Sutter Street, succeeded in building a business and establishing a reputation as a major fashion house of international format.

   Urban context. The site is located about halfway between Willis Polk's Hallidie building (1918) and Timothy Pflueger's magnificent, terracotta clad *style moderne* high-rise at 450 Sutter Street (1929). This prominent architectural environment is believed to be the new frontier for expansion for a flourishing retail district in one of the premier cities of the world. Polk's Hallidie building was a major inspiration for the exterior design of the Jessica McClintock store, not so much in its appearance as in the attitude of its designer in responding to existing local images of the past by application of

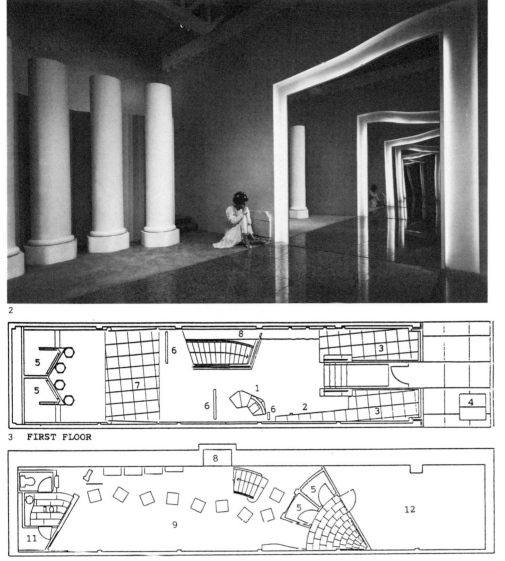

2

5

3 **FIRST FLOOR**

4 UNDERGROUND LEVEL

6 Willis Polk, Hallidie Building, 1918

modern building technology and use of materials of exquisite quality. The style aimed to be reminiscent of the Beaux-Arts movement, by far the strongest influence to overcome San Francisco prior to the International Style.

The store front. The design intends to demonstrate segregation of basic functions.

Decorative element. Use of a single piece, precast storefront element was chosen to be the ornament reflecting the client's image. Glasscrete was chosen as material superior to steel reinforced concrete for long-span cantilevers. The material is a glass fibre-reinforced aggregate of dolomite sand and polyester. Because its major component is produced from crude oil, one may, like other plastics, not consider it a material to be available in the long future. High quality formwork and precasting are a local San Francisco phenomenon due to the survival of an industry which did decorative plaster work in the 1920s and has been able to translate its techniques into large-scale production. Segregation of functions allows reduction of construction time due to prefabrication. The design also intends to demonstrate a further trend towards disintegration of work by various building trades. The artist as construction worker on the site was extirpated a long time ago, but seems to have survived in the yards and factories of even the most advanced fabricators of building components.

Interior space. The store's dimensions are 15×66 feet, yet the client envisioned spaciousness and grandeur. To achieve a maximum appearance of space, three architectural concepts were put to use: change in floor elevation, oversized detailing and creative use of mirrors. A relatively high basement space beneath the first floor

permitted the change to a lower elevation. Architectural details function as decorative elements to accentuate the calm strength of the surrounding space. The concept of interplay between classic and dynamic decorative forms in combination with details derived from undisguised use of materials and supporting systems maintains the customer's interest in the space, directing one's attention along a downward path leading to the underground level and ultimately terminating in the powder room at the far end. Occasional provocative overscaling of architectural objects, almost jeopardising the serenity of the space, suggests that there is presence of larger space beyond.

The 'Mirror Arcade', located where transept and nave intercept in a basilica, defines the culminating centre of the store. The 'transept' is illusionary and appears to be curved through the use of mirrors, positioned at slight angles to each other. Each time light passes through the glass and is reflected by the mirror coating, a shade of green is added to the imaginary space which ultimately disappears from view before it turns into what otherwise would end up being a seemingly endless, unrecognisably distorted, intensely green and faraway ending to the human eye.

Customers entering and leaving the store pass through a stage-like setting flanked by life-size mannequins, neatly dressed and fitted with items available on the sales floors.   *Hanns Kainz*

1 Exterior shows dark silhouette of *Serliana* and smaller rustication.
2 Interior 'mirror arcade' sets up curved reflections as in the mirror room at the Palace of Prince Eugene, Vienna, by Fischer von Erlach. (ph: Colin McRae)
3, 4 Plans show culmination towards the end screen and powder room below.
5 Trusses on dentil frieze hold up screens which repeat silhouette. (Colin McRae)

Hanns Kainz & Ass, Jessica McClintock Retail Store, San Francisco, 1980–81

MOORE, GROVER, HARPER

Sammis Hall, 1978–81, and Rudolph House, 1978–81

Cut-out classicism reminiscent of Palladio, but made with the exigencies of present-day budgets and materials. 'Cardboard architecture', a notion coined by Peter Eisenman to signify the virtual, conceptual aspects which a model can bring, is here achieved for different ends. It is true that the precepts and planning of Palladio are recalled, the dignity and order to which the architects refer, but in a way which may upset purists. What judgements does a Palladian comparison bring? On the negative side one might ask for more substantial materials and craftsmanship; positively there is a light, airiness lacking in the original. The Rudolph House hides its inner dome and then suddenly reveals it changing and back-lit like a Guaraini or Vittone masterpiece. Rhythmical geometries of various abstract whites syncopate on this interior in a way not unlike Palladio's pure colours at San Giorgio Maggiore. Sammis Hall also uses chimneys in a way which recalls its Palladian forebearers in America, and again they mark a central space which is hollowed out and threaded through with cut-out screens. Here the comparison with Guarini's domes is more direct as light blocks break up the overall shape. Back lighting and light used as a rhetorical and sculptural device – with elements of sfumato and chiaroscuro – also unite these buildings.

CJ

Sammis Hall, Cold Spring Harbor, 1978–81

A part of the Banbury Conference complex, Sammis Hall is a 16-bedroom building for scientists attending several day or week-long research seminars. The bedrooms, also used as study and private retreat, surround a sky-lit, two-storey miniature 'Great Hall', or rotunda, which will be used for small discussion groups as well as an informal living room. The hall is enlivened by sets of abstract arches which frame the main stair and float below the skylights. Pairs of bedrooms are entered from a buffer hallway and share a bath.

The site is a large, landscaped Long Island estate. The main approach to Sammis Hall will be axial on a walking path between two rows of gnarled, old apple trees. The design has responded to this implied formality by using symmetry and by using Palladio's inspiration to achieve a suitably dignified image.

Moore Grover Harper

Rudolph House, Massachusetts, 1978–81

The clients asked for a small house with overflow space for visiting children and grandchildren. The house is primarily for summer use. He is an historian teaching at a New England college.

The site is an open meadow, sloping to the west, accessible from the south, and offering views to the north. The topography of the site and the view suggested a direction of movement from south to north on the site, and this direction became an axis about which the design is organised. The geometries of the site and house coincide along that axis and exist elsewhere in a strong relation to each other. The house and immediate surroundings are like a man-made island in the undisturbed sea of meadow.

Inside, an entrance hall opens into the living room and gives a glimpse of the swimming pool and views to the north. The living room is central, with a double wall of enclosure and a dome suspended below the roof of the house. The double wall is derived in part from structural needs but also accommodates a fireplace and chimney, storage, kitchen appliances, and bookcases. It also heightens the sense of separation which is desirable in a small house between otherwise adjacent spaces. Daylight enters the top of the house through dormers and is reflected between walls and dome; it is only reflected light which illuminates the living room with its books and paintings.

To the east of the living room is the kitchen, with a small sitting area (for guests to visit before dinner, without being underfoot) and beyond it, in the pavilion at the corner of the house, a dining area opening to the pool and taking some identity of its own from its ceiling. To the west of the living room is the master bedroom, with dressing rooms and bathrooms. Studies for the clients occupy the pavilions at the corners of the building. Bedrooms and baths for visiting children are downstairs on a floor which opens to grade on the west side of the house.

Beyond the house to the north are a pool and terrace from which a long view opens up the valley towards the north. A formal planting of fruit trees extends up the hill from the terrace, and a cutting garden for flowers is located to the east of the kitchen, out of sight but close at hand.

Moore Grover Harper

1 Section and plan of Rudolph House on longitudinal axis
2 Andrea Palladio, Villa Foscari (Malcontenta), Veneto, 1558–60. Interior vaults are indicated by a curved window and the plan organisation is indicated by a central projection. Palladio combines this clear organisational logic with some Mannerist touches such as the heavy cornice, the broken pediment and upward pushing window (ph: C Jencks)

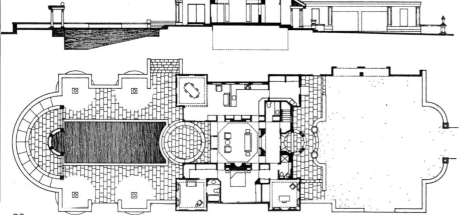

3 Sammis Hall north elevation

4 Sammis Hall west elevation

5, 6 Sammis Hall ground plan and upper floor plan

BEDROOM

BEDROOM

VESTIBULE

BEDROOM

BEDROOM

MAIN HALL

DN · UP

BEDROOM

BEDROOM

UP

BEDROOM

BEDROOM

BEDROOM

BEDROOM

DN

BEDROOM

BEDROOM

MAIN HALL

BEDROOM

BEDROOM

DN · DN

DN

BEDROOM

BEDROOM

7 Guarino Guarini, San Lorenzo Dome, Turin, 1668–80. Ribs and cut-outs give back-lighting and, incidentally, a Hades face repeated eight times in heaven. Spatial layering of this kind has been achieved by Moore in many projects of the 1960s (ph: Thomas Gordon Smith)

8 Sammis Hall, Serliana cut-outs in large centre space
9 Rudolph Hall, 'dome' and 'ribs'

10 Sammis Hall Serliana focused on entry
11 Rudolph House from entryway

12 Sammis Hall from south east   13 Rudolph House porch entry treated as a collage

CHARLES JENCKS

Garagia Rotunda, Cape Cod, 1976–77

This small studio is located in a part of Cape Cod that is unique because of its beautiful fresh water ponds and their connection to the ocean. Wellfleet and Truro are particularly appreciated for the various types of swimming they afford – salt water in the ocean, and the salt can be washed off in the warmer clear water of the ponds nearby. Every day one walks back and forth between ponds and ocean, a pine forest that is dense and enclosed, and the sandy beach of the ocean, which is wide and open. As a result certain images and metaphors stay in the mind connected with purification, the bleaching of the sand, and above all the various blues of the sky and water as they change during the day.

It was this aspect of changing, purifying blues which I have tried to represent in the ten shades of the colour which covers the frame of the studio. As one watches the gateway (or porch frame) throughout the day, dark blues become light, the relative density of each switches place, and the lighter hues actually look darker than the dense ones, especially when they're in the shade. This can be quite extraordinary at times, particularly when a wooden member suddenly disappears altogether into the blue background of the sky. At these moments the sky is captured by the building and taken into its composition (or, conversely, the frame is lost).

The studio is a mixture of two different languages and in this is characteristic of so much Post-Modern architecture in general. The basic shell is a prefabricated garage (although it was finally hand-built) that is basic to the Cape Cod vernacular. The Shingle Style, the roof pitch and many of the catalogue elements, such as the garage door, are local to the area and therefore cheap and easy to obtain. But the Cape vernacular was also chosen because it is understood by the local inhabitants and builders. It's their language and, since I was away when the building was constructed, thankfully so. No supervision needed, no working drawings, the basic shell cost $5500. The idea of the vernacular, that one can specify a building verbally, or in Moholy-Nagy's dream, order it over the telephone, was pursued with varying degrees of success. The most obvious failures, the mistakes and deviations from the rudimentary sketches, were then decorated. It was a Modern architect who said, disparagingly, that 'decoration always hides a fault in construction,' – and so it should. Here ornament, balusters, paint, a pelmet at the rear shaped like a face, cover the mistakes (while also working in

symbolic ways which will not be enumerated).

In addition to the vernacular there is a superimposed language which is quite alien to the area and has more to do with the painted Carpenter-Built houses of San Francisco than the Cape. Queen Anne revival, the elaborate gateways of Michael Graves and the preoccupations with layered space also influenced the design. On the exterior the approach is ordered in a general S-curve, and one proceeds into the building through a series of space cells (see plan), turning at right angles until the centre is reached, with its cross-axis marked on the floor. This focuses on exterior views. The sequence of framed spaces provides a degree of privacy and surprise, but also a framed view of pine trees and scrub oak – the greens and browns which are then bordered by thick blue rectangles.

The inside space is modulated by surprising variations – at least, unusual for most garages. Windows are sometimes on the floor to pick up views under the bushes; a baldacchino-like space is formed by the garage door and steps, and rhythmical harmonies are formed by the studs. The standard 4×4-inch stud is partly used decoratively here and painted in varying shades of blue on its sides to underline the 3/9/5 rhythm of the side walls. The sides, rather than face of the studs, are painted in more saturated hues of blue as they approach the internal corner, and this, to dramatise 'the problem of the corner' (for which there is no classically correct solution) is painted to resemble a mirror (with a dropped stud). Thus the trompe l'oeil of a mirror is used to heighten the facts of construction and the fault in reality. Furniture is also made with the 4×4-inch stud, again painted various blues on the side to distinguish major from minor components; the structural element is made redundant and over-expressed as in a Miesian or classical structure. The garagia rotunda has its rotunda, finally, on the outside where it orientates to the major cardinal points. The four horizons are taken in by the steps which mount towards the centre; the dome is, however, smaller than Palladio's, only one inch high; not only because this is cheaper, but also because domes should be reserved for sacred (or at least public) buildings. As far as possible the normal vernacular is present, but extended by another language. Basically the attempt is to speak on two levels at once, to two quite different groups of people or the same person in different moods in a way that is coherent and suitable to the buildings.   CJ

1 Entrance gate seen from above

2 Plan

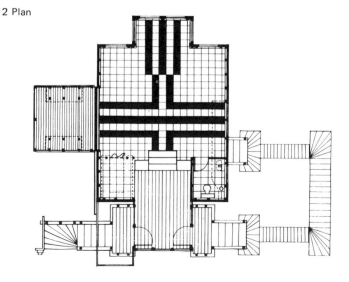

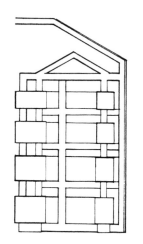
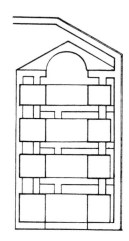

3 Aedicule with 'quoins' used as shelves to hide books and clothing. There were formal incongruities introduced by the decision to put quoins, which graduate in size towards the bottom, on the 4x4 inch 'column'. The main functional problem was to allow the passage of a sliding screen to the right side, while the formal logic would seem to suggest symmetrical quoins. The solution adopted, (lower right in diagram) shows several logics combined, among which is the billowing curtain.

4 3-9-5 rhythm of the wall rectangles is created as a result of using the 4x4 stud horizontally. The internal corner, made from several 4x4 s and a void of 4x4, is then painted as a *trompe l'oeil* of a mirror to intensify the classical 'problem of the corner'.

5 Sun K'o-hung, 'Stretch of Forest Rocks at Snowy Lodge', 1572. The scholar's retreat into nature is a conventional theme of Taoism. (Avery Brundage Collection, San Francisco.)

6,7 The 4"x4" Stud Chair Studies. The problem was to design a chair and table to be built from the same structure as the studio — the 4x4 — and built by a house-builder. This series shows several alternatives explored — to the final result (bottom centre) which was built. The final result mixed 'quick logic' with comfort, cost and function — perhaps too quickly (the chair is not altogether stable). The virtue of 'quick logic' as a design tool is that it allows discontinuous logical assumptions to be developed cumulatively and with speed. (The cushion is also based on the 4x4.)

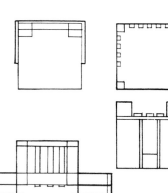
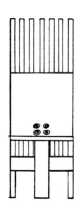

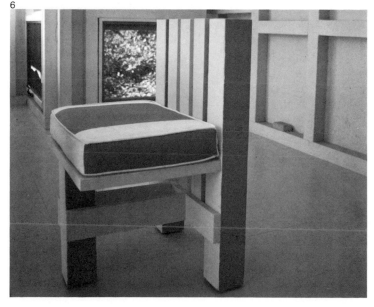

Charles Jencks, Garagia Rotunda, Cape Cod, Massachusetts, 1976–77

JAN & JON

House Jessheim and Digerud Flat

Jan and Jon, as they call themselves, combine aesthetic systems often seen to be incompatible – the classical and Cubist. As they have stated elsewhere the aedicular idea, or 'type', is transformed in many contexts and then collaged in a free-flowing space inspired by paintings of the 1910s. Here we can see in their work a 'triumphal arch' used as a room divider and bookcase; a broken pediment inspired by the Villa Aldobrandini used to organise two halves of a house; and silhouette screens derived from classical portals used to articulate open, office planning. As they point out, the 'type' has to find new usage, continuously, in order to remain a living part of the architectural language. Their freedom in distorting the prototype is partly inspired by the Norwegian Stave Church, a wooden version of the Greek temple and aedicule. Viking architecture, from this angle, can be seen as Free Style Classical. CJ

Some Comments on Free-Style Classicism

'In all of our projects we try hard to draw inspiration from the culture of cities. We would like to transform the owners' ambitions into the ambitions of the city, thus giving individuals the opportunity to express themselves with form to affect space. This is the "participation problem" that concerns us the most.'

Jan Digerud & Jon Lundberg

'Just knowing history does not help: there is no action (it's dead)! However, it becomes alive if it is put into the action of our own time. It is within our power (if we have the ability) to think it anew, to transform it.'

Giancarlo de Carlo, ILAUD seminar, Urbino, 1978

The classical language is not an invention that was made last Monday morning, nor in 1920. As part of our cultural heritage from the start, it has been able to carry complex functions and meanings influencing all of our styles including Le Corbusier.

Louis Kahn's teaching opened our minds again to the possibility that architecture exists on its own terms and therefore speaks to us with a certain autonomy.

Robert Venturi's early works and his fabulous book on complexity and contradiction was somehow a necessary prerequisite for the appreciation of Summerson's short stories on the language of classical architecture. Summerson focuses on the respect for, the freedom of, and the beauty inherent in, the message of this language.

If we are thinking of something worthy of being referred to as a 'type', it is probable that it fits the description of being classical. Because it carries meaning, it is useful today for what it does and its possibilities – not for what it used to be. By definition, a 'type' is special; it is dead in itself, perhaps even stupid. It needs to become specific by being deformed by functional requirements and the imagination of the architect. In perceiving a 'type' as a spatial phenomenon, we end up with the lessons of Léger and Le Corbusier, the ones that re-establish the notion that the spaces between objects are as important as the objects themselves. In fact it is obvious that they meant this in-between realm to be most important – space itself.

To focus on the in-between space-figure it seems more vivid when the silhouette of this figure belongs to something already known, – a 'type'! Be this a teapot (empty or hollow) or a Greek temple.

Dealing with complex functional problems, ornament may be used to make sure that the 'type' is still recognisable. Ornament gives expressive force to a structure. It simply stresses the point that architecture is part of a wider cultural force. The semantic force of ornament makes references to historical styles as it changes in a new context. As an example of Free Style Classicism we once called upon the triumphal arch to solve diverse design problems. Its ability as 'type' to divide *one* space into two zones, without destroying the feeling of 'one-ness' of the original space, was decisive. But this was not enough. It had as a 'type' to solve the function of storage for clothes. Its ability and meaning was not lost by the operation caused by functional requirements. 'The form held,' as Louis Kahn would say.

Obviously we need to start afresh, keeping in mind once again that orginality means having experienced and perhaps understood the original. *Jan Digerud & Jon Lundberg*

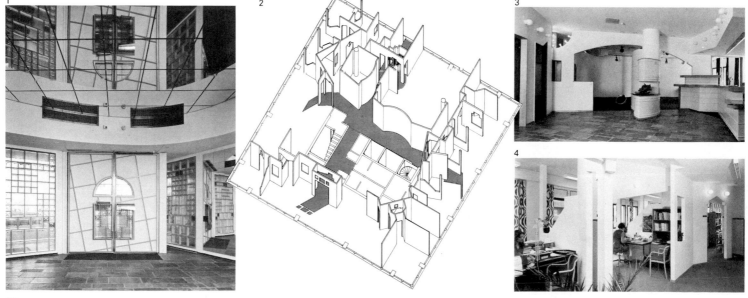

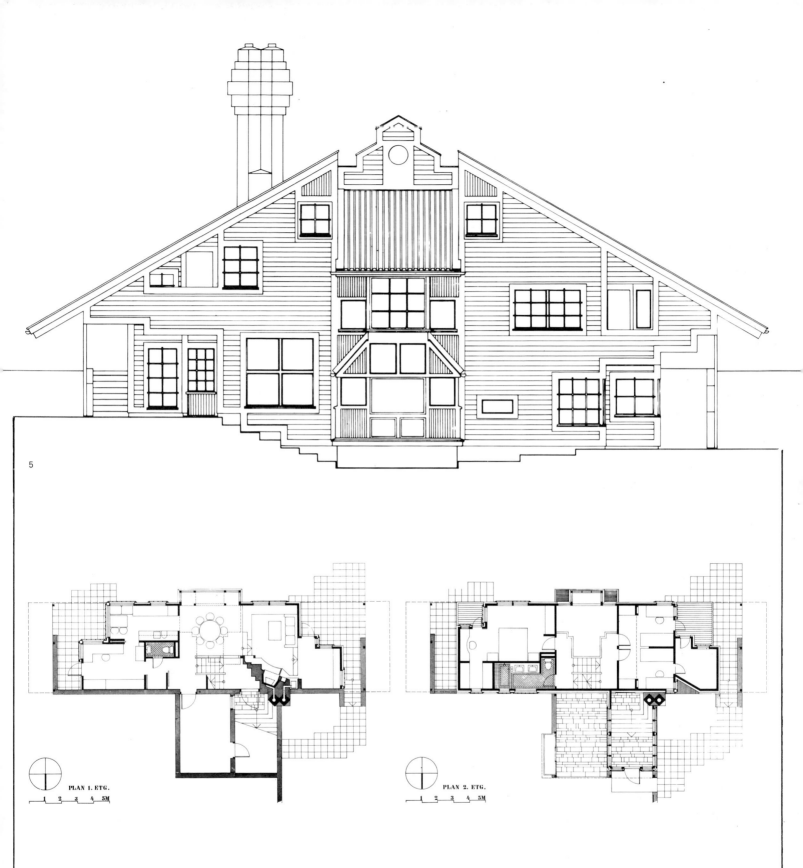

5

PLAN 1. ETG.
1 2 3 4 5M

PLAN 2. ETG.
1 2 3 4 5M

1   Universitetsforlaget (University Press), Oslo 1979–81. Entrance door shows a Cubist collage of classical motifs. Typical office plan shows the 'cardo and decumanus' principle on which are located aedicules and screens. These provide the layering and surprise typical of Post-Modern space.
2   Axonometric drawing by Stian Falck
3   Entrance Foyer shows the telephone kiosk rotated at right angles to the eroded, flattened arch.
4   Sixth floor office shows the overlapping of eroded screens and the cool, white indirect light that Charles Moore and Robert Stern have also used in a similar way.
5   House in Jessheim, Norway, 1980–81, elevation and plans. The long sweeping

roofline has obviously been influenced by McKim, Mead and White's Low house, 1887. Jan Digerud studied under Scully at Yale and his dog is named 'Vincent'.
6   House, Jessheim, Norway, 1980–81. Wood sheathing and decorative wood mouldings are distinguished as in traditional Norwegian architecture.
7   Stairs with Jon below left zig-zag and Jan on diagonal
8   Interior view
9,10   'Triumphal Arch', which is a bookcase and room divider, is used in a conversion of Jan Digerud's Oslo flat, 1980–81. Note the monumental mirror and cupboard in the background which has a 'cut' meant to represent a river and cascade. Art Deco, Baroque and Modern are combined in this illusionistic set-piece.

6
8
Jan & Jon, Norman House, Jessheim, Norway, 1980–81

9
10 Jan Digerud, Digerud Flat, 1980–81

MINORU TAKEYAMA

Nakamura Memorial Hospital, Sapporo, 1978–80

Most hospitals are dull, sterile affairs thrown together, like airports, from a mass of data which may change at the last moment. This one, by contrast, has a monumental integrity and set of subdued images. Classical order and motifs are combined with the anthropomorphic metaphor (see Takeyama's text) and the image of a snow-drenched landscape. Eastern and western forms, figure and background, curve and repetitive square, these and many other dualities set up a dialectic of opposites. Ishii, in the following text, underlines the canonic, rule-giving aspect to classicism, whereas Takeyama, in his comments on Ishii, stresses the popular and academic as well as Japanese classicism. These, according to their testimony, would be the four main origins to the classical revival. Perhaps it is worth mentioning that Ishii studied under Charles Moore at Yale. Takeyama was at Harvard and worked with Jorn Utzon. CJ

This hospital manifests a gradual change in Takeyama's design method. Charles Jencks introduced Takeyama to the international scene by putting the Niban-kan building on the cover of *The Language of Post-Modern Architecture*. This not only influenced Takeyama's development, but also had a great impact on the way other architects saw him. Now with this hospital the stereotypical image of this designer will change. There are quite new elements, among them an allusion to the past, something which has no precedent in Takeyama's previous work.

This hospital accommodates about 800 patients and it specialises in neurosurgery. It's high – 14 storeys – and classical in composition: that is, symmetrical in both longitudinal and transverse axes. The roof, not being flat, can be considered a fifth facade; the walls swinging in and out reflect the ying and yang of architecture. Although the overall design is held together by repetition, it doesn't represent a Miesian solution but rather one similar to those American hotels and apartments that preceded the 1950s skyscraper.

Free Style Classicism, the subject of this issue, I take to be a theme which manifests a conservativism in the overall mood of design, but also one which places classical elements within a Modernist and changing context. This style has gradually developed over the last ten years. In Japan the coexistence of elements from the past and present is not regarded as unusual. In the Meiji period, for instance, this type of coexistence was termed a Pseudo-European style and was applied to many buildings. The older generation of architects placed a high value on this style, and the younger generation today no longer views this as exotic. Their interpretation is that classicism may well be a solution to the present confusion in architectural design. We try to find the potential which exists in a classical design based on absolute rules and theories. *Kazuhiro Ishii*

This neurosurgical hospital, an intense instrument for taking care of 760 patients, has an advanced staff including surgeons and instrumentalists who man their CT Scanners, EEG Tracers, etc. With its medical staff of 500 and two ambulances working 24 hours per day, it typifies today's kind of intensive and proficient dispensing of a health service.

The site is rectangular, facing the 'South 1st Street' one of the major streets of Sapporo. The city was opened a century ago by introducing the American city structure, or grid-iron network. In the distance to the west there is a magnificent view of mountains and a ski-slope, one which is particularly important because it was used at the first Japanese Olympic Games. An antithesis to this is the busy central district and our building, the contrast with a sometimes white landscape.

The content of the building, such as the space quantity, circulation, interrelation of functions, was largely determined by the client, the brain-surgeon, who had successfully pioneered this field of neurosurgery in the old clinic. We proposed, during the design phase, a progressive solution, that is, one better than the old clinic. Our ideas were supported by the medical consultant's and other statistical references. However, no matter how workable they were, the client quite often could not accept them.

This problem was not caused by the client's inability to read architectural drawings. Neurosurgeons can easily decipher drawings and diagrams showing how to operate on the minute details of the brain. The gap between us was caused by the difference in evaluating the function. The surgeons looked subjectively at the proposed functions, through their own experience, while the architect's evaluation was conceptual and objective, or considerate of patients, visitors and surgeons. A convincing excuse for the surgeon's rejecting an idea was: 'Yes, this is a better solution. But it will take some time for us to get used to it and meanwhile we don't know how many lives of patients we might lose!' As psychosomatology says, our hands and body have the power of memory.

The expression of the building survived the preoccupations of the client. Our intention was to establish multiple codes in the architectural language, which could speak to both the medical experts and the patients in the hospital, and to the public and architects outside of the hospital. One of the dominant codes reflects the vernacular language, which was based on the American colonial styles on the one hand, and western classicism on the other. Sapporo was newly exploited and from the beginning the western styles were transplanted in its environmental context. Like San Francisco's Victorian styles, there are good examples of urban classicism which gives a street morphology. This language has become broadly conventional.

The building was symmetrically composed with the 'atrium' on the main axis. We fragmented classical motifs and spread them throughout the building; the roof shape, gable, semi-circular entrance canopy, bay windows, bands on the external wall, interior of the 'atrium', fragmented decorations of the ceiling, and the 'fan light'. At the final presentation, the client associated the shape of the roof with the cerebrum. In fact the patient who undergoes surgery has to shave his hair off and becomes bald. The simile of this sort was not our primary intention in this case, but we expected to depend on the metaphor to a certain degree in order to encourage the popular code of the language we adopted. To appeal to the public we had to alter the preconceived machine image of the hospital.

The external and internal wall was covered with the square white tiles which have three treatments: glazed rough, glazed plain and matt plain surface. Using these three surface effects, we expressed the main syntax of the whole composition. The end wall has a glazed plain surface, the north and south wall have rough tile with bands of glazed plain surface; the matt plain surface surrounds the square windows, and the matt plain surface is in the atrium. The layout was rather arbitrary but consistent. The idea was to highlight the passage of the sun, because this changing expression is basic to the natural landscape especially during the snow-covered winter.

Minoru Takeyama

1

2
3

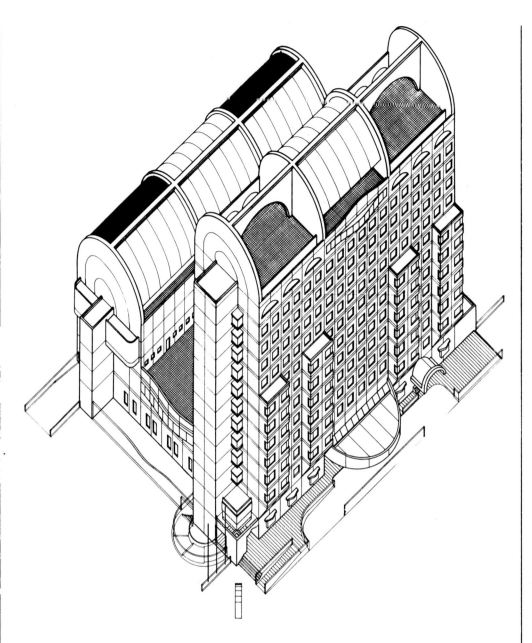

4

1 Elevation from south with lower block for medical treatment in front (ph: Taisuke Ogawa, *Japan Architect*)
2 'The General Hospital, East and West.' *'The East has developed insights into the human body and spirit by analogies and established its own psychosomatic order, while the West has advanced scientific analysis by homologies . . .'* The internal statue represents the body and the patient can find his or her way to the proper place of care by visiting the place on the statue that corresponds to the problem. The cube, a maximalisation of functions, represents advanced medicine.
3 Entrance foyer (ph: Taisuke Ogawa, *Japan Architect*)
4 The building is divided into two blocks; the tall northern block is for patients, the low southern is mostly for medical treatment, including three major operation rooms, examination rooms for EEG, radiology, CT rooms, special labs, etc. The 15-metre long, multi-levelled corridors, with two escalators and the sky-lit atrium on the bottom and the vaulted glass roof on the top, link the two blocks at the five different floors. The lower floors are for public contact; the basement is a garage, the first floor has a restaurant, coffee shops and kiosk, together with a central kitchen. The second floor has the facilities for outpatients. The roof floors, both of the low block (completed) and the tall, are covered with the glass roof combined with the transparent vacuum tubes which are designed to collect solar energy.
5 First floor plan
6, 7 Elevation and detail over entrance

5

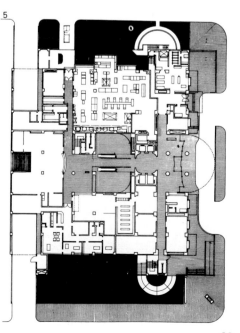

6
7 Minoru Takeyama, Nakamura Memorial Hospital, Sapporo, 1978–80

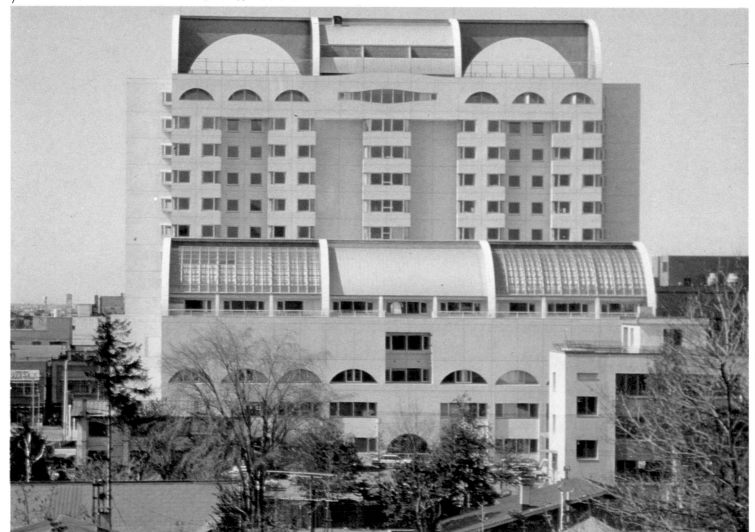

KAZUHIRO ISHII

Gable Building, Tokyo, 1978–80

1   2

3   4   5

This mini-skyscraper mixes, as Ishii states in a tablet placed at the base of the building, the Dutch classical gable with the Japanese Minka roof. It also combines imitation masonry with glass and steel, and at the top a Venturian arch with diagrammatic pediment. The balconies graduate in decoration towards this culmination and thus the eye keeps coming back to the top. Bottom arches are sheared to form an overall figural void, a U- or horned shape, which adds a new dimesion to the classical forms. CJ

Western Classicism in Japan and Ishii's Gable House

Classicism in Japan has always been doubly-coded in its substance, and there exist two contexts of a classical trend. One is the traditional Japanese and the other the Western. Western classicism might be seen as the sign of evolutionary minds, symbolising expectations for the future, instead of recalling our past, by adopting an unseen reality from the untouched Western World. It is not nostalgia for a specific heritage, but a transplanting operation that brings a different form of the same function from a different organism. Not an historian, but a geographer makes this operation. Japanese classicism on the other hand, is a traditional discipline with historical authenticity and authority. Both trends are juxtaposed in the same way as our history – which can be measured both by Christian and Japanese conventional dates.

This juxtaposition had begun as the Shogunate of Meiji finally dropped the reins of government in 1868. When General Takeaki Enomoto, the last survivor of the Shogunal army, disarmed his troops and surrendered to the New Governmental army of Hokkaido in 1869, the second year of Meiji, his troops were fully dressed in Western costume. Enomoto had stayed in Holland to study navigation techniques from a Danish official under the Shogunal mission. There were even some French and British soldiers among his staff. The disarmament took place at a pentagon-shaped castle, the only European-styled one. Contrary to Enomoto's costume, the New Governmental army appeared in very traditional military dress: Kimono with parts of armour on, straw sandals and helmets. All this was incongruously combined with modern shooting weapons.

The dates of both costumes worn at this ceremony were the same. Enomoto's costume was as old as the occupants'. In the immediately following years, the loser's costume was seen as anachronistic and signifying an ultra-conservatism. In fact the New Government, as soon as it restored the reins of government to the Emperor, promoted cultural regeneration and the 'new deal' by encouraging civilians to cut their topknot hair style and give up the sword-wearing custom. Henceforward, Western style became popular in the nation. These conventions of the new, revolutionary custom were not easily adapted to the ruling taste of the public, but rather gradually they became the symbol of the new era.

Environmental phenomena share the same pattern of adaptation with the public. In 1872, the fifth year of Meiji, there was a transplant operation of Western classicism on to Japanese building. A big fire in the heart of the city of Tokyo, where the central station is today, and just on the immediate fringe of the Imperial Palace, provided the excuse for this new style. The city authority had to build a new station quickly, because in the same year they expected to have the first railway connection between Tokyo and Yokohama. A new cityscape and a symbolic streetscape were demanded. They also discussed whether the Western or Japanese style was to exist next to the traditional palace. The final decision was to borrow directly a streetscape from London. A British architect, Thomas James Waters, was commissioned to design a classical British streetscape modelled on Regent Street of John Nash and Hausmann's 'cannonshot boulevard' in Paris.

Two years later, this new Regent Street was realised with slight modifications, and more than 1400 rental apartment units were provided. However, some reactions had appeared among the public. First, the brick wall was not at all conventional among the people, so there soon arose a rumour that a man might catch tuberculosis from getting too close to it. Second, the renting of apartments was not conventional, so that the city office had to change the renting system to home ownership. Third, the inhabitants live differently from the British, so the new form was adopted gradually, while the usage was modified a great deal. Here again Western classicism was not referring to a specific past but to the expectations for an unknown reality which might be better.

It seems that there are two sorts of Western classicism in Japan; one is the style which was transplanted by the authorities, the other is that embraced by the public. The former ruled the official architectural language such as the national Guest House – a direct transplantation of Versailles. The latter influenced mass-cultural taste, and appeared variously in coffee shops and love hotels. In such cases a straight revivalism did not provide the desired effect. A certain modification and even misuse of the original, is often the result of the owner following a market survey. In these cases, the less the architect is involved, the better the result.

Juxtaposed to authentic Japanese classicism, these two faces of Western classicism, straight revivalism and popular classicism, create the immense heterogeneity of the environmental context. Ishii's Gable Building appears to belong to the popular classicism which the Japanese taste culture has evolved, although this is, contrary to what we've said, the product of an architect's effort. The iconographic relation of the building to the surrounding is paradigmmatic, not syntagmatic – instead of repeating or transforming existing street elements, it substitutes an enigmatic image which many people feel they have seen before.

Ishii wishes to avoid Miesian uniformity, or the 'box-with-halls', and to become sympathetic with predecessors such as Sullivan, H H Richardson, even Palladio. These architects shared a common approach toward dividing up a building into its trinitarian parts: base, middle and top. For the skyline Ishii adapted instead of

6

cornice, a Dutch gable which he saw in the US. (The gable reminds me of a Danish country church.) His wish was to add a flavour of 'house-ness' by using this conventional code. For the base, the first two floors, he originally wanted to make three arches. Because of the scale and the main access, he had to eliminate two middle supports and distort the rest as if he were rolling up a curtain. The result gives a better relationship to pedestrian activities on the sidewalk. The middle, containing the rental office space opening up to the street front, was characterised by the fake columns on both sides of the building. The corner looks as if it might have the rustication of a masonry building. The three parts are well linked by the portico which goes through the centre of the facade. It was directly quoted from Palladio's Redentore in Venice, but fragmented and exaggerated in proportion so that it might only be recognisable to an architect.

All this on the facade has nothing to do with what is behind. The facade is a mask, or a costume, for the very ordinary box behind. It is somewhat like a Victorian facade put on a Californian bungalow, but here more discontinuity lies between the public front and private back. A very ordinary pragmatism and common syntactics in the back are shared with the general semantics of the front, but they don't depend on each other. A ready-made building is wearing a new costume, which is not yet adapted to the public taste, but obviously it is the sign of an evolutionary mind within the framework of a conventional morality. Yes, it is even like Enomoto's costume. Otherwise he could have made the dismountable facade which could keep changing as it responded to the surrounding phenomena, or even it was conceivable to have the 'mix and match' book cover on the facade to intensify the meaning of humour to the neighbourhood.

Some might comment on this building that the totality is not recognisable to a pedestrian's eye, or that the scale of the whole being is so misleading that one might say, 'This is Gulliver's house!' Nevertheless, I don't regard this as a misuse of Western classicism. Ishii has presented a successful example of multiple architectural semantics, which can respond both to the public discourse and architects' interests.

Minoru Takeyama

1, 2, 3 Gable building, drawing and views as built.
4   Guild Houses, Antwerp, 16th century (Archer's to right). These Gothic-Renaissance structures show similar dualities to Ishii's Gable Building: arch and pediment inscribed in larger figure, opposition between glass wall and structure, and decorative symbolism. (ph: C Jencks)
5   'Popular Classicism', a private house in Tokyo (ph: Takeyama)
6   Kazuhiro Ishii, Farmhouse in Okayama, 1980. Another gable end accentuated here by an independent frame and top decoration. The 'oni-gawara' is a traditional Asian device which symbolises the devil. Ishii has expanded the gable form to the size of the house and then extruded its form along an axis arguing that such repetitive devices might unify the structure, archetypal house form and village group. (ph: Tomio Ohashi)
7   Gable Building, elevation

7

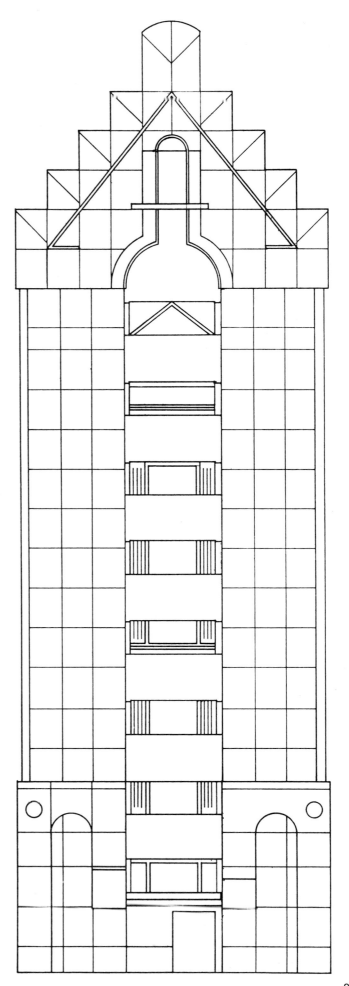

MICHAEL GRAVES

San Juan Capistrano Public Library, 1981, and Sunar Showroom, Los Angeles, 1980

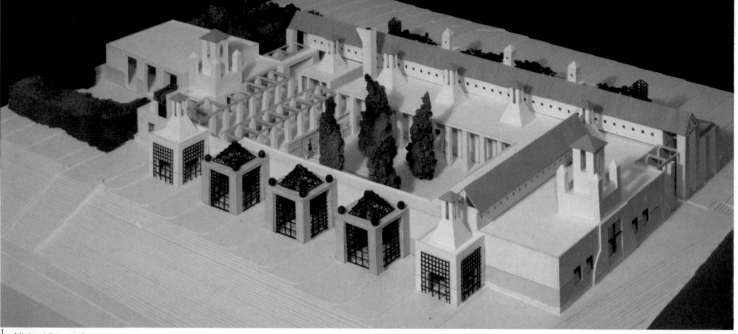

1
2   Michael Graves, San Juan Capistrano Public Library, California, 1980

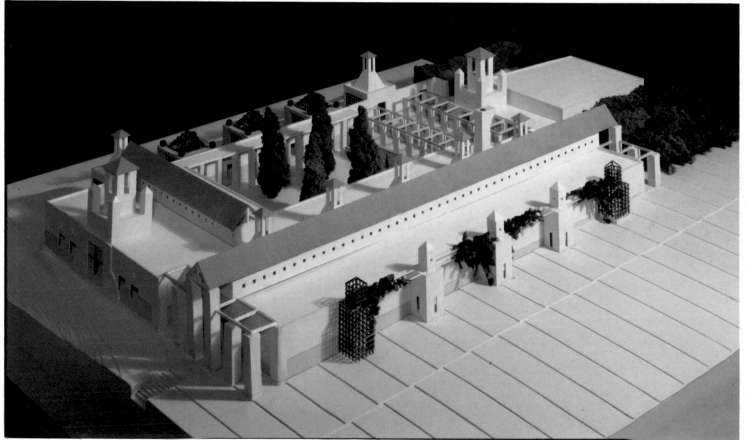

1

Michael Graves, Sunar Showroom, Los Angeles, 1980

2
3

Public Library, San Juan Capistrano

The attractions of vernacular classicism. This scheme, which will probably be built in reduced form, uses certain familiar archetypes in an extraordinary way, so that they always seem to be recalled on the tip of the tongue, but are never quite present. A walled and towered medieval town, an Avila, is crossed with a long, extruded barn with very tiny clerestory windows: an early Christian basilica. Then heavy Egyptian piers – but in creamy stucco – hold up the diminutive, indeed shrunken, truss across the entrance. Pyramidal light hoods, with finials at the four points like a church tower, mark the axis across the courtyard (and the auditorium lobby and story-telling nook below). These also are scaled down from their customary size. By using big forms in miniature, Graves reverses Venturi's amplification: he makes a small scheme seem huge. Is this a monastery or fortified village? Only the cypresses remain unshrunk.

In studying up the local Spanish Mission Style Graves, surprisingly, had recourse to books on Guatemalan architecture. These seem to have inspired his heavy wall architecture, one similar to Barragon's. At the same time, the tiny windows and Free Style Classicism may come from these sources. Of equal importance are the drawings of Leon Krier which have developed the vernacular classical style and Rossi's Modena Cemetery (also in this issue). Graves' ability to synthesise these sources and make them fitting to a public library in a Spanish Mission context is a victory of transformation.

The building shares a front-door entry with a reconstructed stone church. Outdoor and indoor spaces are moulded together in a sequence which gives equal weight to figure and ground. By treating the left-over spaces between buildings as outdoor rooms, and by directing movement towards the entry with a row of cypress trees, Graves manages to dramatise a fragmented and sprawling site. Topiary is used to make the parking area into an archaeological site, the void of his positive library. Movement through the library is processional and measured. Here the Houston Sunar plan has played a role with its linear progressions through parallel colonnades. Three devices are used rather daringly: the shifting focus on cross-axes marked by pyramids and niches; the dense packing where rooms are stacked one on another; and the asymmetrical symmetry where, for instance, one marches down the central nave to find large rooms to the left and filled stacks to the right. Most architects would have been tempted to treat this axial progression symmetrically. Graves has punctuated the space and roof differently to either side so that it syncopates: A-B-A versus C-D-C. The rhythms are held together by the strong nave overhead and the fact that A and C line up on focii. Three such focii cut across the courtyard, the heart of the scheme with its stream and trees, to arrive at outdoor reading rooms. These exist within another

vocabulary of square grey box trellis – just the right contrast to the overall cream and red. With this building Graves confirms the position established by his Portland Building as the major architect of the present. CJ

The building is sited as is appropriate, we feel, not only for its use but also as a part of the urban fabric. We have located the building so that people using the library can enter from the most significant corner of the site, that of El Camino Reale and Acjachema. We have established the entry to be level with grade so that people using wheelchairs will have easy access to the building from El Camino reale. We have also established an automobile forecourt or turn-around on Acjachema, which not only will provide a place for automobiles to drop people at the front door but also will give access to the parking shared with the proposed Mission San Juan Capistrano.

We have further proposed that Acjachema Street be closed to vehicular traffic beyond our proposed forecourt, as a new walk has been established on the former axis of the street to the entrance of the proposed San Juan Mission. We have also proposed landscape elements that help to provide connection between the mission parking lot and the mission entry. It is thought that this parking will be shared by the mission and the library, as the uses do not conflict in terms of the times that these two facilities will be open.

Our building is organised around a courtyard which ties all the various activities of our buiding together into a unity provided by the form of the cortile and the light gained at its periphery. This court also allows us to make thematic subdivisions of the various primary internal uses required in the programme. Quite generally, the adult section is established on the one face of the courtyard, the children's wing on the second, the auditorium on the third, and garden gazebos on the fourth.

One enters the building on the south face, moving along a line which is established by light gained through an upper clerestory. The entrance lobby has a charge desk located on one side and the catalogue table located on the other. Continuing along the axis established by the clerestory light, one finds the reference room, young adult area, and browsing lounge facing the courtyard on one side and the common stacks on the other. *Michael Graves*

1 View of the model from the west with outdoor reading rooms in trellis – little temples (ph: Proto Acme)
2 Public library seen from the east, street side. Note the spine of clerestory windows and the pitched roof which pulls the disparate towers together. (ph: Proto Acme)
3 Site plan with stone church to left, parking lot and shared entrance
4 Sketch of entrance
5 Plan
6 Section north-south
7 *See back cover*, elevations (ph: Proto Acme)

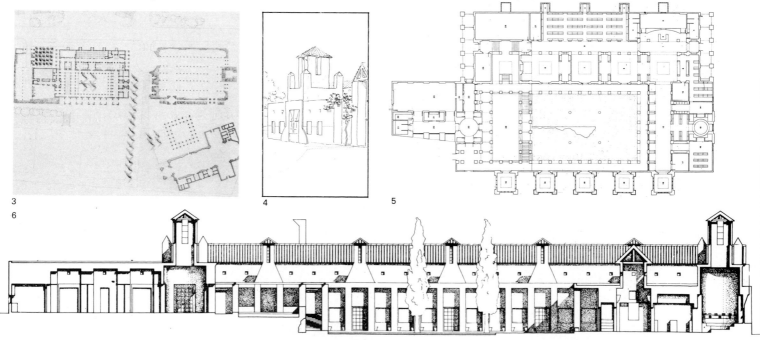

3
4
5
6

Sunar Showroom

A Hadrianic composition made from plaster-coated plywood, cardboard columns, fabric and 35 shades of colour. With this showroom Graves joins the ranks of scenic designers, such as Inigo Jones, who can throw together dramatic background which belie their humble origins and ephemeral nature. Stage sets have often provided a testing ground for later, more serious architectural ideas, and Graves has developed a repertoire of colour and spatial ideas from his five Sunar commissions.

Here certain ironic meanings are intended, such as the reference to the 'Blue Whale', the giant leviathan of Cesar Pelli, which holds this tiny showroom in one of its more awkward corners. Graves has occupied this bungled J-shape with various shades of blue, to acknowledge the context of the whale, and also to create the night sky, the interior, claustrophobic sky (with gold studded stars). A walk through the showroom may be reminiscent of some indoctrination rite into a strange Masonic lodge: is this Schinkel's set for the judgement scenes in the Magic Flute *or the last act of* The Last of the Pharaohs*? It feels vaguely Egyptian because of the squat columns and massive (cardboard) piers – another mortuary temple, the place for embalming.*

Sunar is selling fabric in Los Angeles and an obvious mystery is called for: ironically, most customers prefer to do business in the brightly lit, Modernist end room. Perhaps they are softened up by what precedes it: one entrance apse in night blue, one silver pyramid-shaped ceiling where the textiles are shown. Then, across the corridor, a barrel vaulted rectangle, a gold-ceilinged pyramid, a blue-cylinder hinge space (with a Graves relief showing the basic good things in life – house, food, fabric and architecture), a blue-grey courtyard with ochre pillars, another hinge, another pair of columns and – finale – the anti-climactic Modernist space – to display 'office systems'.

If all this sounds melodramatic, then it sounds wrong, because the formal expression, although rhetorical, is kept basic. Graves has learnt from Leon Krier, Aldo Rossi and Robert Venturi, three architects he admires, the lessons of deadpan rhetoric. His columns are basic. Heavy red ('earth') base; thinner ochre ('stone') shaft; thinnest triangular blue ('sky') sconce. The syntax reverses the usual flaring of the top, the ornament is reduced to colour and light, the metaphors are known to every culture, there are no refinements such as entasis but there is an obvious basic proportion of parts. Square windows and regular shapes (semi-circle, rectangle, triangle) are placed on a complex, shifting axis. This is the mature Graves style which manages to have it both ways, as commercial drama and pure architecture, and like Le Style Corbu *it is one that is widely emulated because it is well done.* CJ

The showroom is organised to show furniture and fabric in a variety of architectural settings. The rooms and spaces have been designed in response to the furniture of the line so that an equity is established between the object in the room and the room itself.

The fabric showroom acts as a foreground pavilion or gate to the general showroom spaces behind it. Upon entrance to the second floor from the elevator one is offered the option of entering the fabric pavilion, moving through its several rooms to the showrooms beyond or, alternatively, of by-passing the fabric display and entering the furniture showrooms directly. The fabric pavilion is recognisable from the exterior by virtue of decorative fabric swags which are used to heighten one's awareness of fabric and decorative cloth in general.

The colours used in the showroom in general are seen to enhance rather direct landscape analogies and also to develop a new 'edge' or sympathetic tension with the colour of the line and what one has come to expect from Sunar. *Michael Graves*

1 Second entrance to furniture. The void squares ('keystones') focus on a Graves relief. The sconce/capital/light is *in* the entablature. Classical syntax is recalled but distorted. Columns are rigid, without entasis, proportions basic, blocky, powerful (ph: C Jencks)
2 Gold pyramid reception room. Graves' relief shows a trellis, mouldings, house, teapot, fabric and nature – the basic good things of Graves' life. They are displayed as if they were part of Sunar's good life. (ph: C Jencks)
3 Office furniture peristyle. The piers are residues of the wall, as in Albertian theory, and act as transitional space to the more private areas behind. (ph: C Jencks)
4 Entrance to the textile shop shows the basic sign of entry, the column wall, which is painted to indicate the base earth (red brick), centre column (ochre stone) and top sky (blue lintel). All this is set against a sky of gold studs. Note the way pilasters and capital are implied by edge notches. (ph: C Jencks)
5 Plan: 1 Entrance, 2 Fabric Showroom, 3 Foyer, 4 Reception, 5 Office, 6 Office Furniture, 7 Domestic Furniture, 8 Office Systems, 9 Kitchen, 10 Storage. A Hadrianic set of primary forms on a shifting axis

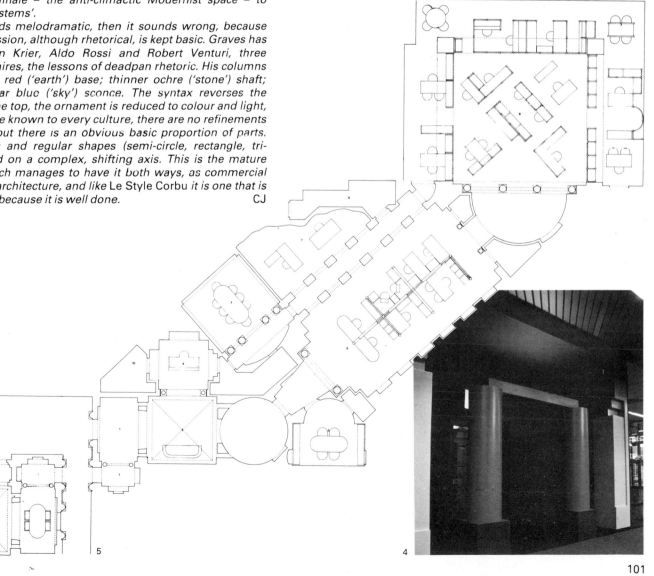

JAMES STIRLING, MICHAEL WILFORD & ASSOCIATES

The Clore Gallery for the Turner Collection, Tate Gallery, London, 1980–84

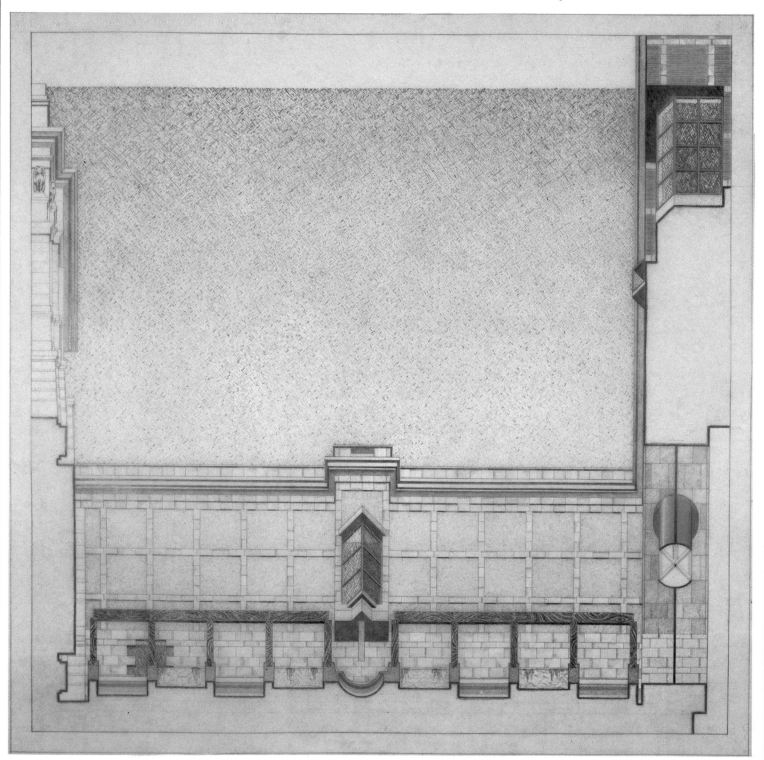

Associate-in-Charge: Russell Bevington
Associate: Peter Ray
Assistants: John Cairns, John Cannon, Robert Dye, Lester Haven, Walter Naegeli, Sheila O'Donnell, Philip Smithies, Stephen Wright, with Property Services Agency, Museums and Galleries Group
Consultant Structural Engineers: Felix J Samuely & Partners
Consultant M & E Engineers: Steensen Varming Mulcahy & Partners
Consultant Quantity Surveyors: Davis Belfield and Everest
Consultant Public Health Engineers: John Taylor & Sons
Consultant Landscape Architect: Janet Jack

1 Up view of garden/riverfront elevation with central viewing window and pergola and seats at terrace level. The parapet string courses connect with, and have the same profile as, those on the Tate

2 Up view of rear elevation facing towards Vickers Tower. Louvre controlled windows to the print collection room and studio glazing (north facing) to the conservation department at ground level. Glazing canopy over tailboard level shipping and receiving service entrance

3 View of model (ph: John Donat)

4 Beehive tomb entrance, Mycenae

Literal eclecticism. This extension to the Tate Gallery takes its cues literally from the surrounding context, then modifies them to a subdued, squared-up geometry. From the right side the brick invades the infill panels, from the left side the stonework, cornice and colour of the Tate fills up the panels. In back, for servicing and contrast to the more public front, is very late Bauhaus Modern, just where it ought to be. To make the contrast more piquant, Stirling has run some of the facades around the corners so that they can fight it out on a single wall. The 'dumb' literalness of these contrasts annoys certain critics who, mistakenly, term it 'pastiche', or 'jokey modern' (Colin Amery). Wilful logic it may be, but certainly not jokey. Like Stirling's work of the 1960s, it has an uncompromising bluntness in parts – it doesn't seek to ingratiate – and this quality has raised doubts in the past. Thus it is presumably meant to do so here.

5 Lutyens' Page Street Housing,1930

The building's very simple L-shape has absorbed a variety of elements. Most prominent is the eroded pediment over the revolving door, a juxtaposition of elements that recalls the 'Treasury of Atreus' at Mycenae. The stonework here and 'oddly' proportioned segmental window relate to George Dance's Newgate jail, as well as directly to the Tate's stonework opposite.

To show breaks and transitions Stirling has used several Modernist compositional techniques. He ends the infill square bays with a quarter beat and then elides them into the next theme; or he suddenly cuts them away abruptly, thus providing the typical Late-Modern 'non joint/joint' – a rhetorical figure that Isozaki has perfected. Indeed the main, voided pediment is an example of the cut-out approach; one that is unthinkable with Neoclassicism or any of the Classicisms save Free Style.

A clear separation of surfaces to accentuate depth and function is allowed by this method. For instance the square glass wall is sunken back twice, at the entrance and corner public reading room, to become a reference plane which unites similar activities – in this case, a view of the garden. The most unusual and therefore controversial aspect of the whole building is the treatment of this

corner. Four odd things happen at once. A funny window pivots out (shades of Marcel Breuer's Whitney Museum?). The brick infill steps up to the right and then suddenly jumps over space to hang. Brick hanging. The glass wall behind chamfers back to avoid these falling bricks and the entablature quickly changes sex.

As if to tone down this wild set of incidents (and one must remember they all have functional and contextual 'justifications'), Stirling has united them into the lines and volumes of his addition. To object to this picturesque symbolism is to object to a tradition stemming from J C Loudon. Of course it has often produced conventionally ugly buildings, but then they are meant to compensate for their lack of harmony with lots of truthful character. That's what we have here – and it's also a beautiful building in its parts. Several notable things are happening at once. The building purports to be a classical addition to a classical set-piece, but as we've just noted it's a Free Style Classicism, or one handled with a picturesque surface and an eclectic set of details. If the symmetry is being kept by the Lodge on the river front, right, and its counterpart to the left, then the Stirling addition would call for another compensating one to cut off the left-hand street – if one were

6 Detail of entrance, model (ph: John Donat)

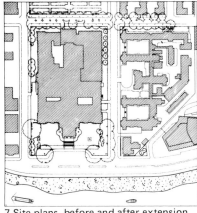

7 Site plans, before and after extension

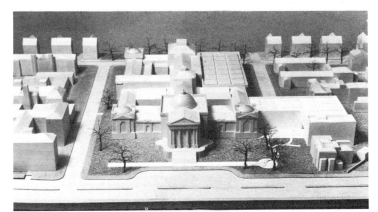

8 Site massing model (ph: John Donat)

following straight classical precedent. This will probably not happen, and it is not in the proposal.

There are several precedents for this asymmetrical symmetry, and Stirling mentions the model of the garden building added to the big country house; but one can still have doubts. From afar the totality will create the impression of a balanced body with one lopsided wing. Closer however, the way most people will experience it, the volumes and surfaces will work in the 'conversation' he mentions. They will respond one entrance to another, one shape and texture to another.

Some of the most interesting aspects concern the sequence of spaces. After we have gone through the Mycenaean pediment and low entrance lobby, the space shoots up in an L-shape (recalling the plan) and focuses through a tall window, in the direction of the galleries on the upper floor. The hollowed-out space is very tight, economic, Mannerist and dramatic – a rectangle which then shifts to the right under a cantilever. Now the erosions of the infill panels and their surrounding quoins really work rhetorically to slice the space, as they themselves are sliced. By running over the volumes, not at the edges as in classical aesthetics but elsewhere as in

Wrightian aesthetics, Stirling can show the square wall pattern as an ordering system, not as substance. Like a Renaissance application of pilasters, this square 'order' is conceptual rather than real structure: the cantilevered pattern makes this clear.

Finally, the culmination of the route, the Turner galleries, is the excuse for the whole design. These are top-lit and indirectly lit with light bouncing off the centre scoops as in Aalto and Kahn's recent museums. In section they may remind us of Roman ovens or medieval kitchens, but as built they will provide an eerie glow of white light that is modulated with sfumato. A single external window, and view of the river, is thoughtfully provided for relief from this unremitting experience of art and architecture. After this feast of vintage Turner and Stirling the cultural gourmand will relish it. The beauties of eclecticism are those of flexibility, variety and depth. An eclectic building of Borromini can respond to various opposite buildings in a site, can change character, even mood, with different functions, and relate fully to a complex, cultural past. This the Clore Gallery, the first major cultural commission in London since the National Theatre, will do.

Charles Jencks

The Clore Gallery for the Turner Collection will be the first element in the development of the Queen Alexandra Hospital Site for use by the Tate Gallery, and it was essential to position the new building in a way that would not inhibit further development. Certain visually important buildings of the Hospital complex are to be retained and integrated with the new building. The Lodge on Bulinga Street/Millbank will be retained. At the moment it is used by the Ministry of Defence and, when available to the Tate, will be ideal for garden functions and tea rooms, with offices and VIP accommodation above. We will also retain the Hospital entrance building on Bulinga Street which may overlook a future sculpture garden and be used as a library/bookshop and for archives. Other remaining Hospital buildings are to be used for offices and storage. The retention of the Lodge with its counterbalancing relationship to the Royal Army Medical College to the south-west preserves the contextual setting of the Tate and maintains the symmetrical balance of the Gallery about its entrance portico. Nevertheless, the Clore Gallery will have its own separate identity and be clearly seen from Millbank across the gardens of the Tate. The existing plane trees will be maintained and new lawns laid across Bulinga Street to the Lodge.

9,10 Entrance hall, interior perspectives

The new building is designed as a garden building (extension to the big house) with pergola and lily pool, a paved terrace with planting and sheltered seating. It will be L-shaped with a gallery wing connecting to the existing building immediately behind its pavilioned corner. The shorter wing returns towards Millbank on the line of the existing Lodge. Setting back the new building and matching its parapet to that of the Tate allows the pavilioned corner, with its greater mass and height, to maintain its architectural significance and leaves the symmetry of the Tate frontage undisturbed.

Approach to the new building will be either from the front steps of the Tate or through a new gate in the garden railings to Millbank and along footpaths to a paved entrance terrace. This sunken terrace relates the corner pavilion with the entrance of the new building and will be a gathering place for visitors and, as it faces south, a good place for sandwich lunches. The increased height of the new building (administration floors) adjacent to the Lodge reinforces the feeling of enclosure at the entrance terrace and

complements the pavilion corner of the Tate.

The entrance of the new building does not face towards the river (avoiding competition with the entrance of the main building), but sideways towards the Tate portico/steps and the shoulder of the Tate – an architectural conversation between the new entrance and the pavilioned corner across the terrace is intended. The existing cornice is carried across the principal façades of the new building and stonework details of the Tate walls are carried partially on to the building. The garden façades have panelling of stone with rendered infill (stucco). Towards the Lodge and Hospital building the panels are infilled with brickwork to match the existing buildings. The colour of rendering will be chosen to mediate between the Tate stonework and the brickwork. The height of the pergola on the terrace relates to the Tate's rusticated base. The secondary façades (NE and SE) are in a light coloured brickwork with coloured metal window elements.

The upper level of the new building contains the galleries and these are at the same level as those in the Tate, allowing uninter-

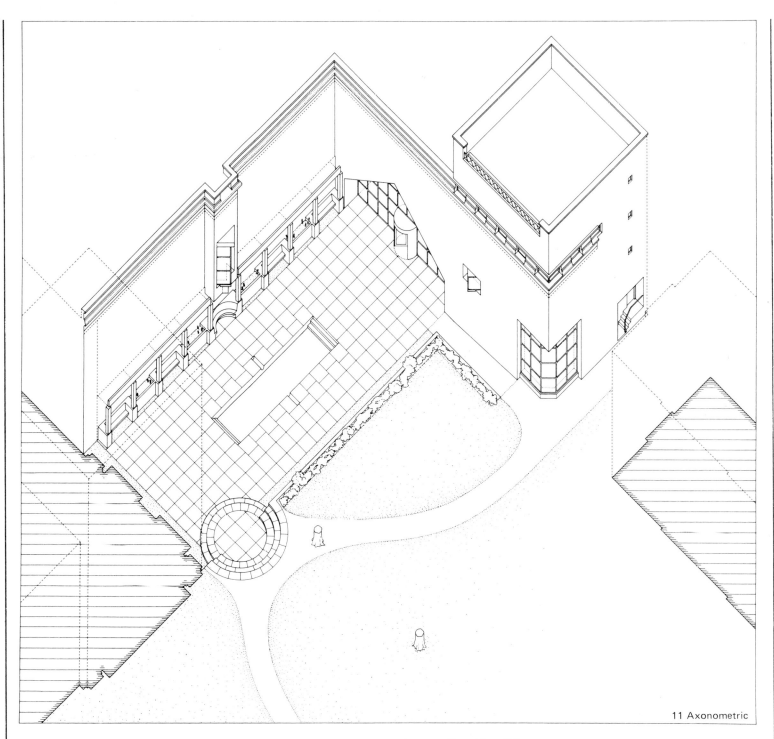

11 Axonometric

rupted flow of visitors to and from the main building. There is a sequence or rooms, smaller and larger, related to the scale and grouping of Turner's pictures. Daylighting will be through roof lanterns. A centrally placed bay window in a small room off one of the galleries is a place to pause, to sit and rest one's feet and enjoy views into the garden and across the river.

Non-exhibition spaces are located at the lower level and include the entrance hall, lecture theatre (180 seats), staff facilities, paper conservation department, plant room, etc. In the entrance hall there is an information and cloaks counter and a showcase containing the Turner relics (his model ships, palettes, glasses, snuff box, etc) as well as the main staircase leading to the galleries. There is also a public reading room overlooking the garden which is fitted with a small servery where drinks and sandwiches can be prepared for evening functions using this room and the adjacent entrance hall, perhaps related to evening lectures. A large lift serves all levels, linking galleries, reserve galleries, print department, paper conservation department, etc; it will carry the largest of Turner's paint-

ings, staff and invalids.

An entrance at the rear of the building serves equally the education facilities in the Tate and those to be provided in the new building (classroom and Lecture Theatre).

As Bulinga Street will be built over only in the area required for the Clore Gallery, the remainder of the street will provide access and parking from John Islip Street. A footpath linking John Islip Street to Millbank will be a continuation of the Bulinga Street pavement through a landscaped area to the north of the new building.

The new building is approximately 3880m². By omitting the paper conservation department, print room and two reserve galleries, it would be possible to build a reduced size of building (approximately 3100m²) if this were financially necessary. The building will cost about £6 million and is scheduled to start on site in early 1982 and be completed in 1984.

James Stirling

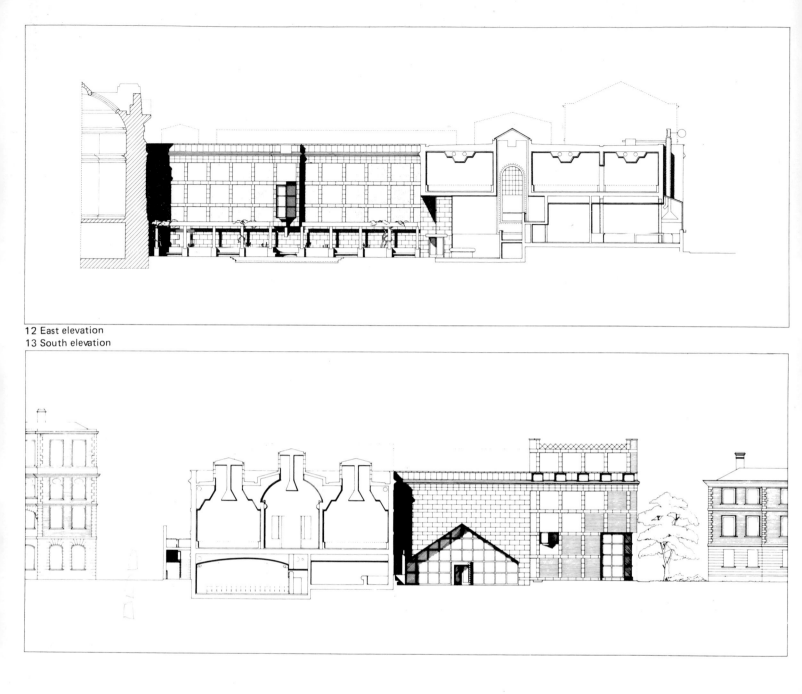

12 East elevation
13 South elevation

14 Ground level plan

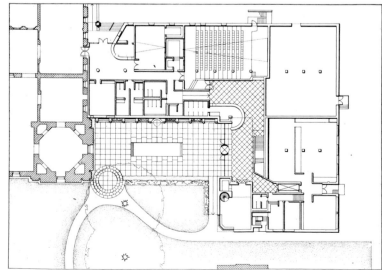

15 Upper level plan

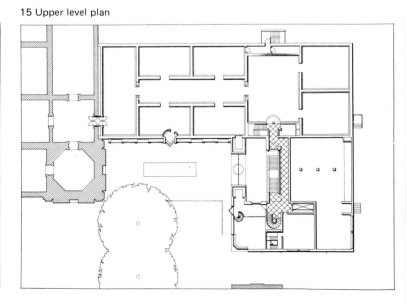

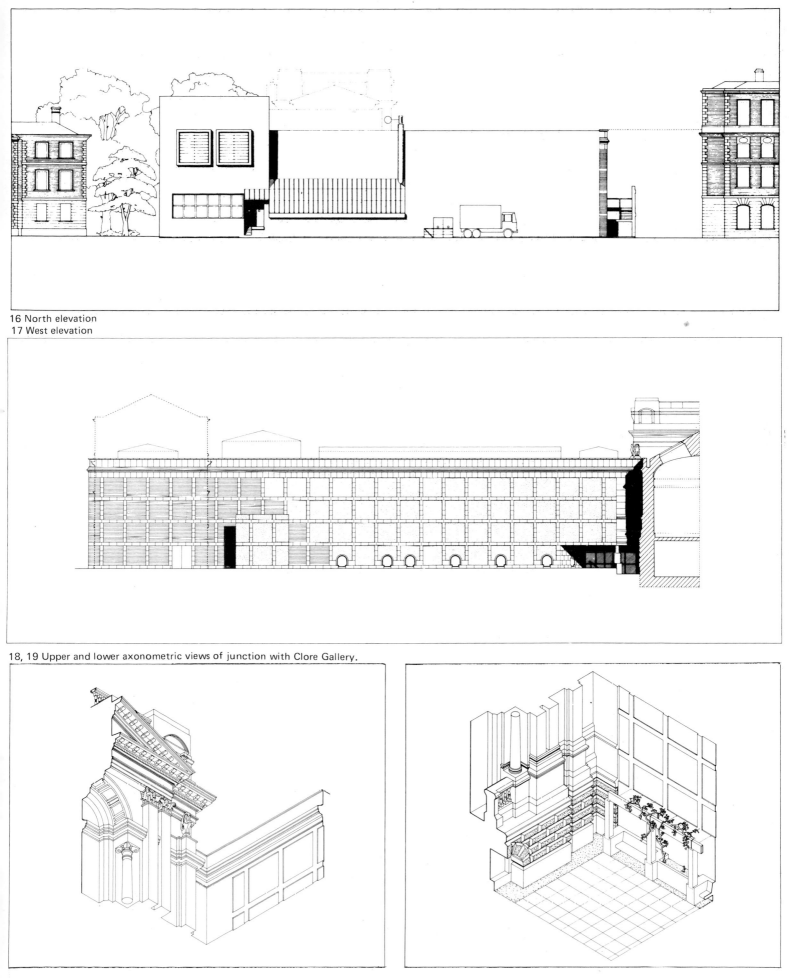

16 North elevation
17 West elevation

18, 19 Upper and lower axonometric views of junction with Clore Gallery.

Charles Jencks

Free Style Orders

The idea of designing a representational Order is as old as the Egyptians. Today the idea has new life, although many designers remain sceptical. James Stirling challenges the notion that a column can be designed independent of context; Michael Graves would have representation kept to the abstract metaphor, and never allow it to become a simile. However much these views may be respected, they have to be set against the benefits that can accrue from regarding the column as a problem in semantics, a place where meaning comes, as it were, to a point. If one can design a representational Order then the rest of the design is easy, because one knows what to represent and the major themes with which to do it. The problems of architecture today are ones of content, not in the first instance ones of technology or form: what is architecture to signify? The answers, or attempted answers, to this question modify the stylistic conventions and technical solutions which both Modernism and Classicism have left us. In a word, the search for meaning pushes architecture to new expressive codes. The Free Style Orders, like the first Doric and Ionic, or like most of the Composite Orders, are motivated by meaning. The new is brought forth by the will to signify.

To this a confirmed Classicist will say 'Why bother? The whole point of the Three Orders is their conventionality and the fact that they don't have to be reinvented. Adopt them as norms and clichés, words of an old language.' To this the Free Stylist answers: 'But the conventions have been broken, the norms lost, the language is defunct, and one of the things which has killed it is hackneyed use. We must design new significant Orders for every city or building task until some are picked as conventions. Then a new language can grow out of the mixture of the past, the present technology and particular culture.'

At this point the dialogue breaks off as the positions seem too distant, irreconcilable and hardened. It isn't until one starts to examine actual practice a little more closely than the protagonists might wish that one begins to see inconsistencies which illuminate the debate. Let us start by looking at an architect who was wonderfully contemptuous of, and very amusing about, designing a new Order, John Soane. He says in his third lecture prepared during 1806–9:

'The *ignis fatuus of Philosophy was the discovery of the Philosopher's stone – with Architects it has been the invention of New Orders of Architecture to rival those of the Greeks. The Romans set the example, and some of the Architects of the 15th and 16th centuries, not satisfied with their fruitless attempts, amused themselves most unprofitably with this visionary phantom of the brain. From then the rage showed itself in France, in the reign of Louis the Fourteenth, where the feeble efforts of the French Architects had still less pretensions to originality and ingenuity. I wish the mania had stopped in France, but the cacoéthes for producing new Orders has reached this country, and we have also had many attempts to attain that object.'*[1]

Soane goes on to mention two examples: one meant to be a Sixth Order 'suitable to the glory of his country', the other 'Britannic Order' is based on ostrich feathers because at the Battle of Crecy the Prince of Wales, after killing the King of Bohemia, ran off with his Royal Diadem which had three such feathers placed on it. After relating more such nonsense Soane concludes: '*I trust these examples sufficient to satisfy us of the imbecility of the attempts, and the folly of endeavouring to produce new Orders of Architecture capable of vying with those of Antiquity*'. He mentions one attempt, as if to compensate for this telling sarcasm, which is 'so

truly in the grand style of Antiquity' (by George Dance) that it *is* a successful re-invention. If we were to generalise charitably from these remarks, we might conclude that Soane outlawed the invention of a new Order, but supported interpretations of the old ones. His own work, however, suggests that it is more complex than that.

If we examine the individualistic columns and pilasters in his own house, or the Dulwich Art Gallery, we can indeed find his interest in first principles and precedent, but it is mixed with the very thing he lampoons: the attempt to design a new Order. The Dulwich Gallery uses the famous Neo-Grec incised motifs to produce 'ghost' pilasters, while brick piers are not so much reinterpretations of the Tuscan as new Sepulchral Orders in their own right. For a tomb they are absolutely fitting. Not only does a simplified sarcophagus crown them, but the blank shadow between, and a stark, wall-like massiveness, imply the finality and stillness of death. We might say this perfectly illustrates our thesis that the new Free Style Orders arrive most convincingly when the architect is in search of a new meaning to express – even though their author, in this case, would have dismissed the idea with a quip.

This tension between innovation and convention may explain the haunting beauty of Soane's new Orders here and elsewhere. That he often followed conventions in a canonic way, and also produced beautiful things such as the Tivoli Corner, is not in dispute. What asks for explanation is the success of his idiosyncratic inventions – his flat domes, layered spaces, odd lighting, all the things for which Post-Modernists admire him – given his strictures and first principles. We might conclude that like so many other Neo-Greek fundamentalists he produced originality through taking orthodoxy to an extreme. He is certainly *the* example, as we noted in the introduction, of the contradiction between canonic theory and Free Style practice.

The more usual case of innovation within a canon, the variations of which Soane approves, are more likely to produce refinements only discernible to the happy few, the connoisseurs or academic designers. That system of classicism is more or less dead for us; we don't have the finely tuned disputes about the marginal variations of Corinthian capitals, which might have engaged architects anytime between the 16th and 19th centuries. We may be able to make the same discriminations, in following their arguments, but they are not very meaningful. Rather the Free Stylists of today are more exercised by radical distortions in the classical code: giving new functions to the column such as electrical, lighting and heating ones; changing the proportions and method of carrying, or deriving new symbolism. (See **2–5**) Michael Graves, for instance, has designed fat, squat cylinders for his Best showroom entry which have neither a real capital nor base. Like primitive menhirs they rise straight from the ground and, in their red shape, they are meant to symbolise the earth – as against the blue-sky truss overhead. The horizontal bands tie them to the ground, divide them into primitive torso and head, and their blank repetitiveness relates them to the Greek Stoa (which they are also meant to symbolise since the showroom is a market place).

They remind me more of those heavy columns found outside of Indian Caves; the heavy shafts which are magnificently decorated with spirals, bands and primary geometric forms. No doubt this will continue to be called Indian architecture, but it probably derives from classical Greco-Roman models and therefore, for our purposes, can also be termed part of the Free Style Classical tradition. Many columns have obvious Doric precedents; the ones illustrated are based on the Ionic bracket, and show a very sophisticated

1
3

2
4

5

6

1 Sir John Soane, Dulwich Picture Gallery, 1811–14. Like Borromini's distortions of Doric grammar, these pier/pilasters with combined base and top have an 'absent' capital, implied by indentations, which then emerges as a 'present' sarcophagus on top. This Sepulchral Order is, like the 'pilasters' upper right, Free Style. (ph: C Jencks)

2 Robert Stern, Ferris Booth Hall, New York, 1981. Lighting piers with sconce capitals have been revived from the 1920s in Graves' and Stern's work

3 Terry Farrell, Farrell Offices, London 1981. Farrell writes: '*The columns provide many functions like transmitting heat and wiring through their hollow core to the floor level, but their prime contribution is visual. Although there are only six, there appear to be more because mirrors are used at both ends. This reinforces the central axis of our three rooms, and the problem of irregularity in plan is overcome by the mirrors. The trompe l'oeil is strengthened by a linking arch set below the capitals. The capitals are globes which provide all the background light to the offices and, for security purposes, are on for 24 hours a day. Their non-structural role is clearly stated by the bright round glass tops and their hollow plinth bases which, in most cases, contain filing cabinets'.* (ph: Jo Reid and John Peck)

4 Robert Venturi, Knoll New York Showroom, 1979. Large, bland light cones, with black neckings, form a neutral background for furniture. The curve is reminiscent of Egyptian and Persian forms and has the 'pretty/ugly' duality beloved by the team which designed it, Venturi, Rauch and Scott-Brown

5 Allan Eskew and Malcolm Heard, of Perez associates, Lafayette Arch, New Orleans, 1978–79. The tensegrity column is still more of an idea than reality although here these architects are getting there. Steel poles become Gothic ribs; stars at the top are cross-bracing capitals, while black steel wires are tuned like outriggers on a schooner. All this supports an 'entablature' (ph: Alan Karchmer)

6 Michael Graves, Best Products Showroom, competition, 1979. A stoa carried by wide, red earth cones, banded to define their waist

7

Fifth Order *of the* Gothick Architecture.   *Plate* **XIII**

8

Batty and Thomas Langley Inv. and Sculp. 1741.

handling of classical themes. Fluting graduates towards the centre portico (now broken away) in steady geometric rhythms which are very pleasing. From square base to octagonal shaft to 32 spiral flutes turning right, balanced on the other side by 32 spiral flutes turning left. The centre columns show the full multiples – 4,8,16,32 – and take these geometric rhythms up in the cushion capitals, or transfer them down to the base (with corner figures that are now for the most part missing and presumed stored in someone's private collection). At the top the bracket capital again asserts the wall plane of the base and, of course, becomes the focal point for Buddhist iconography which will reach a culmination on the inside. Bulging animal heads are set against serene Buddhas; amorous, flying couples give wing to the carrying brackets. The sanctuary front repeats with dramatic representation the overall presense of the cave, which is a cultural icon set precipitously on a cliff above the water – with and against nature.

That classical columns have influenced Hindu, Buddhist and Jain columns and that these have, in turn, influenced later classical ones is a hypothesis which will not be pursued here. Influences have always travelled back and forth, and in a country house such as Sezincote one can see the designers moving form Greek Revival through Hindu to Muslim and back again, with no trouble. Free Style Classicism was assumed by them as it was by a designer such as Batty Langley. In 1742, he wrote 'Gothic Improved by Rules and Proportions in many Grand Designs ...' By 'Gothic', he means Saxon – in reality, English. By 'improving' Gothic he is really designing a new English, national Order – which he avers is not only as beautiful and rule-bound as the 'Grecian mode', but just as cheap as well. We don't find here the explicit iconography of the Indian columns, but rather a retranslation of Gothic forms into Classical proportions and parts. As John Summerson puts it: *'The Gothic of Kent and Batty Langley was, fundamentally, a free variation of classical forms constituting not an imitation but an equivalent of Gothic.'*[2]

The general proportions of shaft to base, the presence of cornice mouldings, 'metopes' and other classical devices bends the Gothic language back to its progenitor. Gothic was one natural offspring from Roman architecture. Vitruvius was read in the Middle Ages, and Langley is doing something quite logical in trying to make evolution run backwards – as it can in architecture. Before we look at recent attempts to design representational columns, we will consider the most systematic attempt at working out a National Order, like Langley's.

Notes

1   John Soane, Lecture III, from *Lectures on Architecture*, delivered to the Royal Academy from 1809 to 1836; edited by Arthur T Bolton, published by the Sir John Soane Museum, 1929, p 42.
2   John Summerson, *Architecture in Britain, 1530–1830*, Harmondsworth, fifth edition paperback, ed 1970, p 399.

7   Ajanta Cave No 1 (c 660) The colonnade accents the centre (missing) portico with articulations in fluting and decoration. Most of the columns in the 30 caves combine fundamentalist shapes with exquisite decoration, an opposition which reflects the extreme contrasts between nature and culture, site and architecture. (ph: C Jencks)
8   Batty Langley, *The Fifth Order of Gothick*, 1742. Note quatrefoil metopes and classical base mouldings.

A French Order

Charles Jencks on Ribart de Chamoust

M Ribart de Chamoust, *L'Ordre François Trouvé dans la Nature*, Presenté au Roi, le 21 Septembre 1776, pub 1783 Paris

The following text, on the invention of a French Order, was translated with the aid of John Skinner. Quotes from the text are interspersed with commentary.

The Neo-Classical artist, such as Reynolds, often made an equation between elements that to us would be distinct if not opposed. Thus abstraction, perfection, the ideal, the ancient and above all the natural were all bound up together. Classical art was a part of Nature, and thus overcame the schism between artifice and the natural realm, culture and nature. This invention of a national Order, or rather its discovery in Nature and Her Laws, is very much in the Neo-Classical tradition. Ribart opens the first section:

A la Nation . . . . A people desirous of every kind of glory will not be above adding to the Greek Orders a particular Order which will distinguish its monuments, in a manner that is as felicitous as it is new. I say new, not to pretend to be the only one with the idea of a French Order, but because I am really the first who has found the principle in Nature; that is to say, who in giving this New Order all its proportions, its grace and richness which one finds in the Greek columns, has above all applied this character of originality which it must possess.

Since François I, the restorer of letters and protector of arts, many of our august sovereigns have desired an architectural Order elegant and rich which would characterise the nation. De L'Orme sought one for Catherine de Medicis, under Henri II and Charles IX. Louis XIV, who wished that his century would become *the* epoch in the history of taste, as it was in great events, proposed a considerable prize and marks of distinction, to whomever should succeed in this interesting search.

Blondel, Perrault, Girardon, Desgodets and other celebrated artists worked on it, but most of them limited their efforts in varying the Corinthian capital and all of them produced Composite Orders which were more or less bizarre: in effect they forgot that to compete with the Greeks it is necessary not to follow them step by step, but rather go back to primitive theory, that is to Nature itself.

In following the same route, I had not the temerity to believe that my talents surpass theirs; but the beauties of an art depend often on a happy accident. And this accident, which I believe to have encountered, has delivered me as them to search for a French Order. The public will be my judge . . . .

In this description we note the way a French nationalism and glory is assumed as a proper goal to signify, and the Greek Order is assumed to confer a cultural identity on the Ancients which ought to be emulated. This chauvinism and more legitimate pursuit of identity or character marks the invention of many Orders. We might also note Ribart's comment on these inventions that spring from the freedom inherent in the Composite Order, the one which is the most bizarre and free-style of the Five.

In the first section Ribart mentions how difficult it is to invent ideas and forms equivalent to the Ancients, partly because the architect no longer enjoys the social status of a Dinocrates. He discusses an Order as composing a column, entablature and its parts, and how the Greeks perfected them in the year 3536, under Pericles, after having studied the example of the Egyptian Orders. Doric and Ionic were invented from nature. With the Corinthian – 'On y reconnoit la nature, mais supérieure à elle-même' (p2), he mentions the Roman inventions of Tuscan and Composite but warns that a new Order can not be created by changing a few ornaments in the capital, as Vitruvius well knew. For an effective invention:

... It is necessary to go back to the source, to the principles and to the type. I mean by the word *type*, the first attempts of man to control Nature, to make it serve his needs, agreeable to his customs, favourable to his desires. The tangible objects that the artist chooses with justice and reason from Nature to illuminate and light at the same time the fire of his imagination, I will call *archetypes*. (p5)

In Section II Ribart discusses the Greek Type and the question of volumes or dispositions, in general. He rejects the necessity for a columnar order to produce boring parallelopipeds, and argues that a variety of forms can be produced by new plans of columns, thus foreshadowing his strange triangular plans. This argument has an almost Modern ring to it, recalling Buckminster Fuller, the notion of the 'trihex' as an alternative to dull rectangles, and even the ideas of Aalto.

The Third Section, 'The French Order perceived in the Greek Type and its development', contains his most important 'discovery'. Like Laugier with his Primitive Hut, or the first men of Vitruvius imitating the swallows and constructing huts from mud and wattle, Ribart stumbles upon the great lesson of Nature. But of course 'fortune favours the prepared mind', and in the description that follows we can see the author oscillating between discovery and invention, Nature's contribution and his own. Joseph Rykwert has analysed this passage in his On Adam's House in Paradise (1972) *but my translation is somewhat different:*

'I was walking in the shade of a forest on my estate, in a gorge which opened onto the Marne. Some young trees, placed three by three so regularly, although planted by chance, came into my view. The groups of these trees as an ensemble formed the space of a natural room, hexagonal and rather unusual. At this view, my first idea of the changing of volumes awoke, all the more since I saw that it conformed with what I had already thought about the French Order ... Perrault coupled columns and pleased everybody. Why if I put them in threes as were these trees would I now awaken an equal interest since, like him, an increased beauty would result from the harshness and closeness of columns so much sought by the Ancients? On the other hand I will facilitate their separation and openness, for which the Moderns have sacrificed all. I perused this room with a certain pleasure and took it for an archetype ... I imitated the Achaens in their composition of the Doric ... I had the trees cut above, not below, the fork where they branch out. I placed from one to the other the cross beams, and put above them girders, a decking and roof, and I rediscovered truly the Greek type, but with a new aspect and with considerable differences.

The following spring, the tender boughs which showed their heads at the branching of the cut trees formed there true capitals more real, without doubt, than those of Callimacus. Several thick roots naturally coiled about or twisted into the rolling terrain, marked the bases. A turfy lawn made by my miller, beside his wier, made the outline of a stylobate. I thought it needed nothing further by way of ornaments. This type offered me the first proportions of the parts, the union of the columns and their intercolumniation; and I found in these already the new type of mass and its distribution ... The need for an agreeable location to hold the party which Friendship celebrates at my place each year suggesting my choosing this above other spots. I had it decorated with garlands of flowers and it took on the form of a rural Temple dedicated to Love. (p6–7) (I)

Section IV compares the Three Columns with the Three Graces, and leads to that slow, creative unfolding of analogy which we can find in other new Orders whether they are Gothic, Spanish, or American. Ribart stresses the purity of Nature, his discovery of its principles and its 'primitive composition' to which he can add 'brilliance and elegance':

In the three columns of each group I seemed to see the Three Graces, which we always represent as inseparable. I thought what better to model their distinctive proportions on than the stature and positioning of the Deities. I also followed the Greeks in this, who had made the Doric column follow the proportions of man, Ionic of a woman, and Corinthian of a young maiden. The three French columns united, recalled thus to my Nation these three amiable sisters who pour out affability, charm and gaiety on the work of men and the gods. So that one could easily make a comparison of the two groups, I include here the design of a little national monument which I modelled in clay. I thought one would feel these relations better than having them demonstrated mathematically. It is not that I have neglected such proofs as I have calculated; but not everyone would be interested.

Ribart takes great pains later to derive mathematical proportions based on eyesight and perspective, but at this stage in the argument he just mentions the 'scrupulous attention' he gives to the proportions of his Deities as being equivalent to that of the Ancients. Beauty is said to attend such refinements and clearly Ribart's careful drawings and obsessive research testify to his belief on this matter. He goes on to describe a kind of national mythology comparable to that which was being fabricated by other Neo-Classicists, also searching for an equivalent to the Greek myths. (James Macpherson's forgery of Fingal, 1762, and other poems ascribed to the mythical Gaelic bard Ossian, show a comparable motive in another field.) These are Ribart's 'Observations on the Ornaments of the National or French Monument':

The three virgins which dominate the national or French monument are not, for us, of recent date. One can find them in Edda, between the principle deities of the French Celts, our first fathers, under the name of *Urd, Werandi, Sculde* ... I find in the three virgins the *Magnanimity, Affability* and *Generosity* which still characterise the French nation today and which make the whole world desire our domination ... The Samothes ... placed the throne of *Odin* under a spacious ash tree and our three deities entered its perpetual freshness ... Some think they are the Greek goddesses *Aglia, Thalia* and *Euphrotine* as they pretend to find *Odin* in the sovereign *Jupiter*, in *Frea* the lovely *Venus*, in *Thor* the powerful Love, in *Tyr* the intrepid *Mars* and in this way many others. One would be on more solid ground to say, perhaps, that the gods are nothing but the relative emblems of the Empire of Gaul just as they are of the French.

Odin signifies the sacred personage and perpetual rebirth of our Kings. *Frea* signifies the charming majesty of the empire which extends to the extremities of the world. *Thor* is that love between the Prince and his subjects ... This is not the place to decide to which country the Graces belong, and other nations can have their own, but I am content to assure you that those which crown my monument are the French Graces, without doubt the most majestic, the most gay and affable which have ever existed ... (p9)

Ribart goes on to describe the iconography of the three sides of his monument, explaining of the side we see in his engraving that it shows the figure Generosity (III):

Under the second figure of *Generosity* the medallion appears with the words *The Beneficent King* surrounded by olive leaves. From one side is a sceptre with a radiant eye as many Egyptian sovereigns used ... on the other side is the torch of Genius which Louis will relight in his country through his good deeds.

In a note Ribart explains rather proudly that his three phrases – viz Le Roi Bienfaisant *– have 16 letters like Louis XVI. He continues to explain his rigorous iconography with the three bases:*

On the second face a cock stands on a thunderbolt. Nothing could better designate the French spirit. The cock which has a strong heart and proud bearing, could as nobly carry the thunderbolts as the Roman eagle. The vigour of the Gauls is as distinctive an attribute of our nation as it was of theirs ... They took the cock as an emblem, not because of the similarity of nomenclature, but because it called men to work and announced the break of day; and it is always ready for combat, and glorious in victory.

Ribart points up the morals in the other symbols – a little child

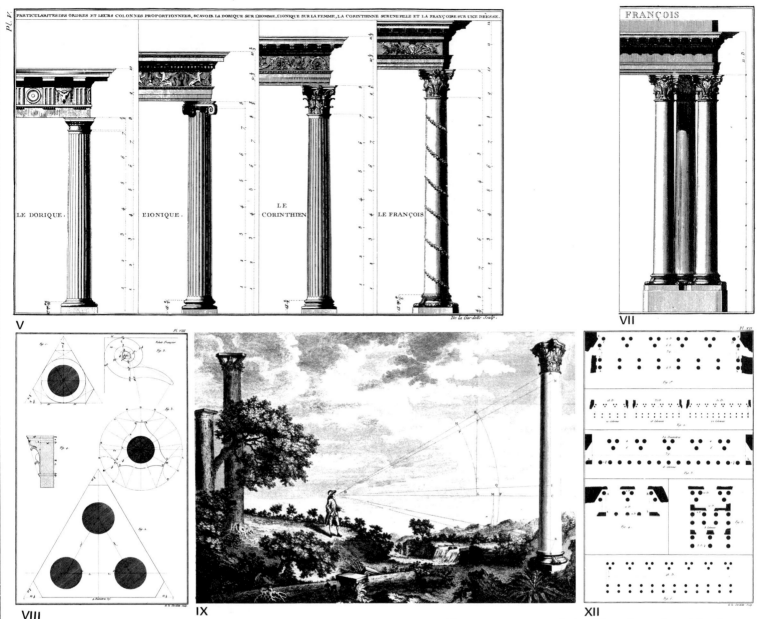

LE DORIQUE.

L'IONIQUE.

LE CORINTHIEN

LE FRANÇOIS

V

FRANÇOIS

VII

VIII

IX

XII

playing on a tambourine earns our nation the friendship of all others – signs of music and dance which also have a beneficent civilising effect. Throughout these descriptions of the three sides we find a moralising exhortation which is his contribution, not 'discovery found in nature'. At the base of the monuments in tables placed on the stylobate are three inscriptions:

APA (Aux Peuples à Venir) Louis by his good deeds reanimates industry, revives the laws and saves the country. ASF (Aux Siècles Futures?) Louis revives arts in their activity, and his people live in prosperity. ALP (A la postérité) Bringing back gaiety, calm abundance, Louis will bring his happiness and the happiness of France (pp10–12).

Perhaps this French Order was never built because of the revolution six years after it was published. Ribart's ideas of royal beneficence and chauvinism might have been hard to take at the time, but it is interesting that he is always careful to tie them to ideals of nature and more general ideals of civilisation.

His next section, V, concerns 'The Particulars of the French Order' and it starts with a typically bold and boastful flourish: 'The French Order is the most light, most elevated and most ornamented of all the Orders. With respect to these virtues it owes everything to Nature, and principally to the Graces which embellished the beauty of the Order.' (p12) *His engravings bear out his boast in several*

respects. The measurements, derived from Perrault and Cordemoy, show a seemingly natural progression towards the French: eg Doric is eight diameters high, Ionic eight and two-thirds, Corinthian nine and one third, and the French hits the decimal – ten – exactly. While the first two orders have 'coiffeurs' or 'crowns', the later two have proper capitals – 'whole heads'. As one can see, the French order is marginally more ornamented, slender and tall than the other ones (**V**).

The base of the French Order, with its inward-turning scrolls bound together by straps, relates to the volutes of the capital, and in this sense sets up an anastrophic relationship which is quite common to Post-Modern columns. Ribart mentions these relationships, the mutual appropriateness of parts, and then allows a poetic conceit:

The heels (counterfoils) which are appropriate to the lightness of the Graces as well as the swiftness of Mercury, seem pressed down by the weight, and this gives the impression of force as well as ornamentation. They are indispensable in this Order because of the accord they give between base and capital ... When I look at my three columns as the three Graces I call this type of reversed consol heels and when I regard them as trunks of trees I call them rolling roots. One can find similar Gothic columns ... and grotesque figures ... I find admissible only that which Nature presents me without violence; I cajole Nature whereas the Arabs outrage it. (p13 and footnote)

Here we have the typical Neo-Classical idealism which extracts what Natura naturans *holds as a possibility, but what* Natura naturata *may not have yet created. As Hugh Honour shows in his book on Neo-Classicism these distinctions were clarified about the time Ribart was writing, and are common to Canova, Mengs and Reynolds.*

Other particulars which Ribart points out include the garland of flowers which makes a spiral of six revolutions, a capital proportioned like the Corinthian to be the head of a young girl, a 'chapeau' at the top of a three-sided abacus with a knotted ribbon (**VI**) *(not the usual sun or rose) and, most striking of all, in place of the acanthus leaves, the three* fleur de lis *of L'Ecu de France. Each flower has two side flowers and two oval volutes which resemble those chopped off branches of his original model (p15). Ribart goes on to distinguish his creation from others which have been well-studied, such as the capital of the Temple of Jerusalem (reconstructed by Villalpanda and others).*

His entablature of two diameters is lighter than the other Orders; the architrave and cyma have profiles which resemble the Temple of Peace in Rome 'which has always been thought elegant', he says, citing Palladio and Desgodets. The frieze has ornaments which portray the majesty of the French kings, or the grandeur of their empire, or the gaiety of the French spirit. The cornice resembles the Corinthian of the Temple of Mars the Avenger in Rome. 'The lily is the greatest of flowers', Ribart assures the reader and he ends this section with an apostrophe on its virtues including its 'suave smell' and the thought that since he has found the archetype and its true principles 'his success is certain'.

Section VI, 'The French Order, the Fourth Order, taken from Nature and demonstrated as much by primitive principles as by the proportions' contains a discussion of Doric shafts, canonic columns such as those of the Pantheon, and a host of expert opinion including that of Pliny, Vitruvius, Palladio, Scammozzi, Serlio, Vignola, Barbaro, Cataneo, Alberti, Viola, Blondel, Perrault and French academics. This chapter not only assures the reader of the writer's erudition on the matter, but also allows him to point out why his predecessors failed: 'because they stopped their research with different models, which they did not regard from the point of primitive principle and which they did not base on precepts of a taste sure and truthful'. (p23) His primitive principles lead to the necessity of the French Order coming in threes, which he illustrates in another comparative engraving. The way the three shafts grow slowly apart from their common base gives the upward movement a rather paradoxical visual force as the thin intercolumniations themselves grow upwards (**VII**).

Section VII, 'Rules and Measures' contains minute descriptions of layouts, triangulations, spiral curves, etc, and the proportional system for diminishing the column. Here again Nature is the guide. Trees, like Greek and Roman columns, don't swell out as they grow upwards, 'an absurd idea', but start to diminish about one-third of the way up. So with the French Order which is also based on the natural science of optics and the viewpoint of the observer with his eyes off the ground. This relative vantage point naturally generates a natural proportion and diminution. (p33) (**IX**)

Section VIII concerns 'The French Peristyle and its Intercolumniations', four mathematical 'demonstrations' that his triple columns are not more expensive than the single colonnade because they do not necessitate a greater number of columns in totality. These wonderfully specious proofs, the Fullerite mania for triangulation and economy, result in comparative plans where the columns may be counted by the sceptical (**XII**). *Sections IX and X are rather perfunctory examinations of the rest of the French Order – the doors, lilies, balustrades and pilasters which harmonise with it. Section XI concerns 'distribution', the new kind of geometrical figures which can arise from the equilateral triangle used as a fundamental element. Lozenge and hexagonal plans are the main types which are new. Section XII, 'De la Bienséance', on decorum, argues for the appropriateness of the French Order when applied to edifices of a grandeur and magnificence beyond the ordinary. Temples, theatres, city halls, law courts, triumphal arches, palaces for princes or governors are the obvious building tasks. Ribart avers that since the French Order is superior to the other three it ought to be consecrated 'to Divine and Eternal Wisdom, to the Universal Creator, to the Sovereign who is Master of the Heavens and Earth' not to a mere pagan god to which the Greek Orders are dedicated. (p50) He designs his Temple of Divine Wisdom, Ste Sophie, with the French Order and works out all its 'French' relationships* (**XVII**). *On the high altar is a majestic figure of Divine Wisdom, saying 'It is by me that Monarchs reign with glory and equity in the heart of their subjects, it is by me that the legislators order that which is just.' She holds in her right hand a brilliant lamp, perpetually burning 'where one can see the form of a tetrahedron ornamented with several Hebraic characters on each one of its faces; in her left hand is a serpent, emblem of eternity and at her feet is a sphere where one can mark the accord and harmony of the Universe'. Here again we are reminded of the universalising aspects of Neo-Classicism, and in particular of the primacy of the sphere in representing this universality: the spheres of Goethe, Ledoux, Boullée, the young Vaudoyer and many subsequent designers at the École. The Resumé, the last section and one unluckily numbered thirteen, restates Ribart's faith in having 'found this Order in the book of Nature emanating from God'. The ornaments, without profusion, have a 'noble simplicity' which was, by then, 1783, a Neo-Classical cliché. The discovery of the Order seems to have been reserved for the glorious reign of Louis XVI, named "The Benificent" and Ribart ends his book with the unmistakable idea that there is one way in which Louis can show his great beneficence. Alas, it seems never to have happened. This treatise on the creation of a new Order, although worked out in more detail and with more semantic cogency than any other that I know of, fell on barren ground.*

Pl. XVI

Charles Jencks

Representational Orders

The idea of representation in architecture is faintly ridiculous – like programme music which seeks to represent thunderstorms and the brotherhood of man. One won't find many serious architects concerned with the matter, although they may touch on it in passing. Usually they say one or two things about 'appropriateness', make a few nods in the direction of the Three Orders and their semantics, and then consign the whole question to another profession like sculpting, or the gentle art of billboard painting. The question of *explicit* meaning in architecture has been given the silent treatment for reasons which must be too obvious to mention: it's vulgar. One remembers Cecily's great mistake of calling a spade a spade, which got Gwendolyn's retort: *'I am glad to say I have never seen a spade. It is obvious that our social spheres have been widely different'.*

The architect who goes around labelling his parts is in as much danger. *'Always suggest, never name,'* is the social and aesthetic injunction, *'if you want to rise above the Philistines who are always telling you more than you want to know. Or if you must label then, like Magritte, be sure to get it wrong.'* Art and architecture thrive, indeed depend, on the mysterious and enigmatic for their appreciation: naturally, then, on the priesthood of critics who will decode the cryptic set of messages. And writers who don't like this state of affairs, like Tolstoy, go mad and pen distempered and embarrassing books which have labels called What is Art? (What is it for Tolstoy? The infectiousness of feelings transferred through a medium and understood by all – or at least 'normal people'.) Clearly between Tolstoy's populism and the more common approach today of art for the happy few (or a specific 'taste-culture' as it is democratically expanded) there is nothing to choose. Art, and the public art architecture, must be, at one and the same time, comprehensible and obscure, totally explicit in certain of its meanings and only open to those who will take the trouble to explore it. Such an obvious truism only needs stating when the partisans of populism or elitism momentarily get the upper hand. It follows from this rather undevastating conclusion that representation is a necessary, if modest, part of the architectural obligation, and thus we may fruitfully explore various attempts to make explicit Orders.

The Egyptians produced quite an array of symbolic columns which varied from those based on three plants (the papyrus, palm and lotus) to those based on generic types (bud and bell capitals) to those based on anthropomorphic parts (the Head of Horus, the body of Osiris, etc). All of these quite explicit signs were stylised and then incorporated, even subordinated, to a syntax of continuous stone elements: eg, fat 'cheese-like' base, swelling 'trunk-like' shaft, 'fountain-like' capital, 'chunky' entablature, and 'gorge' moulding. The syntax and semantics kept a basic parity. Anyone looking at these Orders is aware of their metaphorical qualities and harmonious articulations.

The Greek columns, which developed directly from the Egyptian Orders, were by the fifth century less explicit semantically and more harmonised syntactically, but a symbolic role was still present. With the caryatids especially, as described by Vitruvius, one has quite explicit attempts to symbolise such things as the 'shame' of Caryae and the fact that the women were married (hence the 'long robes'). Caryatids, and Persian slaves which carried loads on their heads, were 'burdened with the weight of their shame' which sometimes showed in their pained expressions. But for every Atlantes who struggles under the weight of architecture, there is one who carries it effortlessly, or with joy, or with no expression at all. The point is that sometimes the symbolism is detailed and specific and other

1 Jean-Jacques Lequeu, Symbolic Order for the Hall of States in a National Palace, Paris, 1789. An allegorical Order meant to crush the counter-revolutionists and have their 'shame' made eternal, like that of the caryatids. The irony of the Lords holding up the Peoples' Palace on their heads must have appealed to Lequeu. He described the frieze having *'demons with fleurons, interlaced with scrolls of foliage, fitted out with rifles, pistols, swords . . .',* but these are hard to see.
2 Robert Stern and Robert Graham, Column with Figure, New York, 1981. Not visible from this view is the fact that the Ionic column is cut in half and that the figure looks about to make a one-and a half gainer. The asymmetrical steps behind are not, as they look, a symbol at a Russian trade fair, but a statement about the divided and hybrid times in which we live.

times it is general and aesthetic. The constant, opposite pressures on architectural expression – semantic versus syntactic, specific versus general – can indeed be seen as antagonistic. Architectural quality is a result of interweaving these demands so that they are all present, not necessarily reconciled.

Jean-Jacques Lequeu, more than other architects of his time, was interested in the visual simile. As a result many of his buildings look quite mad to us, especially as we have different symbols. And they look very ugly, as will any architecture so devoted to symbolism. Several of his inventions are disquieting in a Surrealist way and, at the same time, are well worked out on a syntactic level. His 'Ordre Simbolique, de la Salle des Etats d'un Palace national' adopts several classical conventions of the herm: the half-figure, half-shaft, supporting, 'unhappily as a Persian slave', the capital on his head. The proportions of column, figure, entablature and the transitions with mouldings are all within well-tried conventions. Thus it is only the peculiar features which stand out symbolically: the chains of the aristocrat's enslavement, his French garb and downcast eyes. Lequeu very effectively highlights just those parts of the message he wishes to convey. As his own caption says, these columns 'represent the aristocratic Lords, those fugitive despots, their accomplices and subalterns, all criminals against the nation, who are now enchained.' Other explicit meanings are absorbed in the frieze.

Robert Stern and the artist Robert Graham have produced a column with a figure surmounting it again according to well-established conventions. This Order, exhibited, at the Architectural League in New York (an institute which played a role in the 'American Renaissance' of the 1890s and its classicism) is obviously symbolic – but of what? *'Human scale arising from the ashes of Modernism, and Late-Modernism in back,'* was one way Stern put it in a lecture. *'It expresses my own confusion,'* was another aside, the confusion about today's classicism. The Ionic Order is cut in half so that the rather squat column and its classical pedestal are, as it were, challenged from behind. This back has chrome verticals descending on an Art Deco staggar, a reference to very recent set-back skyscrapers, among other things. On the top an aggressively sexual amazon in bronze seems ready to spring, as if from a diving board. The weight is on her toes, her posture is alert. At the same time, like Stern's generic column, she seems like a generalised female – perhaps even the illustration in a biology handbook. So she is symbolic of such abstract notions as 'human scale', and we can indeed read the Order as showing the juncture between Post-Modern Classicism and Late-Modernism, with the implied triumph of the former. We can also imagine exponents of the latter responding to her posture shouting, 'Jump, jump, jump!'

It is one of the problems of explicit symbolism that it may elicit such uncharitable replies. All emblems can have their meaning reversed, whereas abstract figures cannot be blasphemed. This may be one reason the Modernists developed non-figurative columns. They were certainly against literary meanings, or metaphors that became so explicit as to become similes. Le Corbusier allowed that he designed the *pilotis* of the Unité d'Habitation like the thighs of a strong woman, but he only *said* this, not expressed it with formal cues. Pier Luigi Nervi used plant analogies for his large piers at the Palace of Labour, Turin, but again he suppressed details which might have made these meanings more understandable. With Frank Lloyd Wright's 'lily-pad' columns at the Johnson Wax Building, the simile almost comes out, as we look up to see the ripple of water overhead. This illusion is created by the sparkle of many pyrex tubes bundled tightly together. The image, however, is combined with other metaphors. We can see the small 'shoe' at the base, the reverse taper as in a Cretan column, the top 'necking' like an Egyptian capital, and so the simile competes with others. For Aalto, Mies and Gropius the story is much the same. They start to develop an Order, with an explicit syntax and semantics, and then suddenly stop short; or rather quickly go on to something else. the result is that Modernist Orders, such as they exist, are rudimentary, primitive, underdeveloped, when compared to the Free Style Classical ones (eg, Egyptian).

We can, however, play a semantic trick on these designers and group their creations according to a system of oppositions, so that they constitute a gamut. Let us invent the 'Six Orders of Modernism' and group them according to their semantic properties. Unquestionably Gropius' 'pole' is the most primitive Tuscan. Mies' cruciform pier with its diminutive capital is the heroic Doric, just as Le Corbusier's strong thighs (the next in line) have a similar, severe masculinity (in spite of his feminist claims). Aalto's Wolfsburg order is clearly the middle-aged Ionic woman that we all know about, slightly dumpy and with attached ribes acting as the robes which signify marriage. Then comes Nervi's elegant Corinthian and Wright's even more slender Composite, the very height of eclectic charm. Conventional proportions and the actual colours of these columns may go against this reading, but no matter, we could 'improve' them.

This exercise reveals at once the primitiveness of the Modernists and the fact that they were concerned with syntactic, not semantic, matters. Some of this work has unquestioned beauty (Wright), or expressive force (Nervi, Le Corbusier), or constructional honesty and purity (Mies), or idiosyncratic charm (Aalto) or a disarming dumbness (Gropius). But it takes the whole problem of representation, the wonderful challenge of architecture as a symbolic art, the great game of 4000 years – and gives up: 'Leave it to the billboards, the cinema, the caption-writers and audio-visual talking guides – *anything* as long as we Modern architects don't have to face the indignity of designing explicit proletarian messages.'

Things have thawed a bit since this puritanical ice-age and a few architects such as Venturi, Stern, Moore and Graves are beginning to think about the Orders again. They aren't yet ready to design full frontal representations; or when they do they are hedged around with veils of double meanings, ironies and the like. But one can predict that the logic of the situation may soon force them to try. In any case, to aid in the birth of this next perilous stage of history I have had students design these dangerous emblems. Some results from Pomona and UCLA in Los Angeles, and the Architectural Association in London are shown by way of conclusion.

The design could be for a National Order à la Ribart, or one for a city, or place, or function, or idea. The only desideratum was that the student found it significant. To prepare for their design, to make up in the hot house of the Academy an evolution that usually takes 200 years, they were forced to copy one of the Three Canonic orders. They were then asked to colour it incorrectly, in a non-canonic manner. After this violent bit of indoctrination followed by iconoclasm, they were told to search out a Free Style Order and copy that: eg, Otto Wagner's heating units of 1905. This they were allowed to colour correctly. Then they were ready for their own design. But first they had to write a description; they had to start with a programme, with content, before they could find fitting forms. The Final Judgement was a jury in which other people had to 'read' some of their intentions.

The difficulties encountered were the obvious ones of explicitness: caricature, pastiche, overemphasis. To counter this the usual Modernist values of syntax and technology were restated with the added idea that the work must have personal, ambiguous levels of meaning quite difficult to untangle. No one achieved a perfect fusion of these conflicting demands, and not enough explored new technologies, or a new syntax. But some were creative, others witty and a few actually understandable – as intended.

Students at Pomona, UCLA, Los Angeles and the AA in London designed representational Orders based on locale, ideas or functions:

3   The Six Orders of Modernism. Left to right: Walter Gropius, Ukrainian State Theatre, Kharkov, 1930; Mies van der Rohe, New National Gallery, Berlin, 1962–68; Le Corbusier's Unité d'Habitation, Marseilles, 1946–52; Alvar Aalto, Cultural Centre, Wolfsburg, 1959–63; P L Nervi, Palace of Labour, Turin, 1960–61; Frank Lloyd Wright, S C Johnson & Son, Racine, Wisconsin, 1936–39. To make these Orders complete their proportions and colours would have to be 'improved'. (Drawn by Thomas Schregenberger)

3

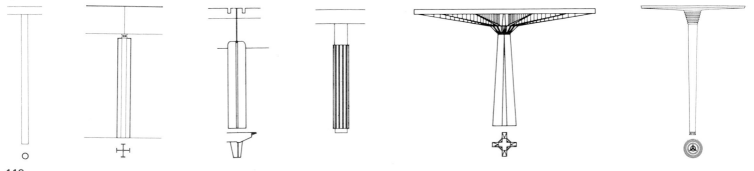

4 Joe Vetrini, The New York Order: 'The base is a rusticated cube representing the ''skylump'' buildings so popular at the beginning of the century, while the two tunnels recall a view so familiar to New Jersey commuters. The shaft symbolises the two most famous ''skyprickers'' ever built, the Chrysler and Empire State Buildings; the entablature is made from the initials of the greatest city in the world; and the N, with its extended legs, symbolises the twin towers of the World Trade Center (which reaches the highest point on the entablature). The Y represents a workman in overalls, and the men whose determination built the city. Thus the comparison with the masculine Doric order is obvious. The faces are painted in the colours of the various races; the American Indian is finally acknowledged to have played a part in constructing the city. The various ethnic groups form the unique ''melting pot'' of New York. Under the arms of these workers, whose proud heads will not bow, and who reach as high as the tallest building, is sheltered a relative newcomer to the famous skyline – the Citicorp. All the proportions are based on those of the Doric.'

5 Jeff Blechel, The LA Order: 'This column represents Los Angeles growing from and supported by its freeway system. The freeway is the link between the city of skyscrapers and the green lawns and palm trees of suburbia. The coastline reinforces this connection, while the sunset, at the top, is one of the most attractive aspects, not only of this column, but of LA.'

Aside from the explicit references one can detect an upside-down keystone, the column as giant billboard or sign, and the whole thing as an illuminated lamp. The LA overtones thus are tied with the explicit cues.

If this all verges on the edge of cynicism, then the next designer has intended to go over this edge and express a contempt for LA. Paradoxically however, the negative meanings can be read positively. One of the beautiful aspects of architecture, when given a syntactic rationale, is its ability to express more than it intends.

6 Ken Knott, The Californian: 'This column represents another step in the evolution of the Corinthian Order, and it takes its direction from Victorian columns. The volutes have become dragons (because of the Chinatown influence) and the anthropomorphic face found in Victorian work has become a skull (Hell's Angels). The acanthus leaves remain as a design motif, and as a reminder of the Corinthian influence.

7 Ken Sutter, A Composite Column with Ionic Volupts: 'Los Angeles is a strange admixture of culture and kitsch. How important is surfing except as a symbol: one symbol of youth to bear aloft, another symbol of youth? Or are the surfboards really rockets? Los Angeles boomed with the aeronautics and space industry. Remember the happy story of the engineer Howard Hughes who designed a faithful support structure for Jane Russell's volupts? Here there are of course references to nature also – citrus and vino. All this is surmounted by a celluloid coronet of the silver screen. The base anchors the column in the Los Angeles freeway system and nourishes it on fast food.

'The proportions are about 1:6 – which is squatty and crude, but a safe slenderness ratio for an earthquake city.'

8 Jeff Sessions, House of R Royce: 'The design of this column was influenced by a drawing of the Pacific Design Center used metaphorically as an architectural moulding. The House of R Royce takes large, readily recognisable Los Angeles buildings and attempts to reduce them to abstract architectural images of base, shaft and capital. Nearest to the ground is the softened-box base of the manufacturer's Bank Building. The undulating surface treatment and the varying progressions of the horizontal courses of floors is suggestive of a glass and spandrel rustication. Above this the twin fluted shafts of the Century City Towers support the jewelled crown capital of the Bonaventure Hotel. The PDC appears here also as a moulding in the architrave and frieze, which then supports the cornice, pediment and roof of the new Crystal Cathedral, complete with a hood ornament acroterion.'

4

5 6 7

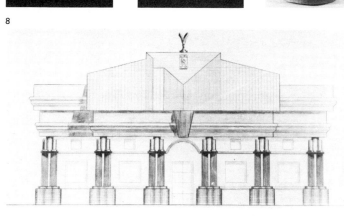

8

9   John Drew, Butterfly Column: 'This column is for a museum of butterflies situated on Exhibition Road in South Kensington, London, not too far from the Natural History Museum - which has similar columns (see below). The principle idea is taken from an event which occurs on the island of Rhodes. Visitors and tourists come to what is known as 'the Valley of Butterflies' and they watch the guides who beat the trees and bushes with their long, thin sticks. The air is suddenly filled with butterflies.

'The column represents one of the trees. Around the base are bound the guides' staves (which recall the Roman fasces, or symbols of power and authority, and the less pleasant aspects of this form of butterfly collecting). The tree is twisted foretelling the twisting columns outside the Natural History Museum – which is next on the route. There are 14 turns since each butterfly and caterpillar has 14 segments. The capital of the column has a butterfly on each of its four sides and, as a cushion for the entablature, the head of a giant pin. This is a premonition of the pinned collection. The columns also show the life cycle with the egg (ovum) at bottom, caterpillars crawling up the twisted bush, cocoons suspended under the capital and the butterfly emerging triumphantly (for an instant) at the top.

10   Mojca Svigelj-Cernigoj, Money Order: 'Coming from a society, Yugoslavia, where money is a means to an end, I found America a place where money has become the final goal. It is a society, I feel, in which people are almost paranoid about making it – that is, making as much money as they can.

'If such a society were to erect a temple, it might be a circular one with a colonnade encompassing an inner glass prism full of coins and bullion. In this temple the colonnade, with its tight intercolumniations, makes it hard to slip through. On the opening day of worship, a tragedy occurs: the first ones to arrive try to squeeze between the columns, but most of them get stuck. More motivated ones try to climb up over the twisted bases, reach over the slippery part, and climb the steep staircase. A few lucky ones make it, find the hole and walk in. For these there is light everywhere; brilliant, shining, gold.

'But there are also signs that the structure is not as strong as it should be. The triumphal arch can no longer carry its load, the columns are shaking and twisting; yet no one believes that this world monetary structure will not survive. The column is made from stacked coins: silver quarters, nickels and dimes for base and capital, and copper pennies for the shaft. The column proportions are 1:6:3 and the intercolumniation is ½ a diameter.

Like several other designers Mojca was initially motivated by certain ill feelings and these led, in the first instance, to a rather ugly caricature. After a few discussions this changed slowly. It was pointed out that architecture, particularly temples, tend to last for more than one generation, and that this Fort Knox could not afford to have a single meaning, whether positive or negative.

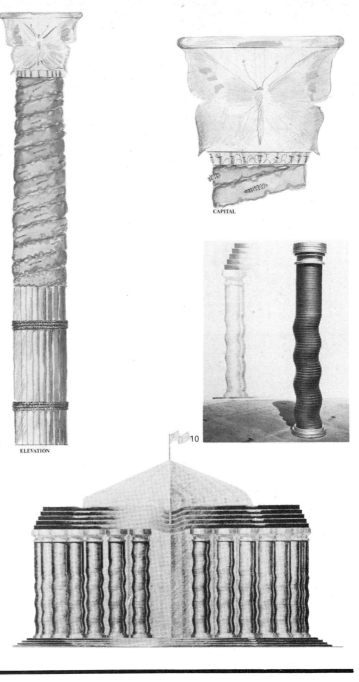

CAPITAL

9   ELEVATION

10